Ex Libris
Jean M.
W9-CTW-763

SARAH JOSEPHA HALE

SARAH JOSEPHA HALE

The Life and Times
of a Nineteenth-Century
Career Woman

Norma R. Fryatt

HAWTHORN BOOKS, INC.
Publishers/New York

Grateful acknowledgment is made to the following: Massachusetts Historical Society for permission to quote from a letter dated February 24, 1830, from Sarah J. Hale to Gen. H. A. S. Dearborn; Vanguard Press, Inc., for permission to quote a letter from F. Hodgson, reprinted from *Happily Ever After* by Constance Burnett, published by Vanguard Press, Inc., copyright © 1965 by Constance Buell Burnett; Mount Holyoke College Library for permission to quote from a letter by Emily Dickinson, dated November 6, 1847, to Miss Abiah P. Root; Princeton University Library for permission to reprint a letter dated August 6, 1973, from Sarah J. Hale.

SARAH JOSEPHA HALE

Copyright © 1975 by Norma R. Fryatt. Copyright under International and Pan-American Copyright Conventions. All rights reserved, including the right to reproduce this book or portions thereof in any form, except for the inclusion of brief quotations in a review. All inquiries should be addressed to Hawthorn Books, Inc., 260 Madison Avenue, New York, New York 10016. This book was manufactured in the United States of America and published simultaneously in Canada by Prentice-Hall of Canada, Limited, 1870 Birchmount Road, Scarborough, Ontario.

Library of Congress Catalog Card Number: 75-2559

ISBN: 0-8015-6568-5

1 2 3 4 5 6 7 8 9 10

If we mean to have heroes, statesmen, and philosophers, we should have learned women.

Abigail Adams

Contents

Acknowledgments   9

1   East Mountain Farm   11

2   A New Home and a Wedding   15

3   Sarah in Boston   24

4   Help for the Shipwrecked   32

5   A Special Piece of Ground   40

6   A Gain and a Loss   50

7   Publishing in Philadelphia   58

8   Women Invade Literature   63

9   A New Era   69

10 Education for Life, Not "Nonexistence"   78

11 A Healthy Body   84

12 Inequities or Iniquities?   89

13 Marriages and a Festival   95

14 Peaks and Valleys of Popularity   101

15 Gleams of Light in Darkness   111

16 The Storm and Its Aftermath   120

17 "An Enviable Immortality"   133

Appendixes   140

Books for Further Reading   145

Index   147

Acknowledgments

In addition to those institutions and sources cited elsewhere in this book, the author wishes to add a special thanks to Carnegie Library, Rockport, Massachusetts; Sawyer Free Library, Gloucester, Massachusetts; Hobart & William Smith Colleges Library, Geneva, New York; Richards Library, Newport, New Hampshire; and descendants of Sarah Josepha Hale in Texas and in Clinton, Ontario, Canada.

1

East Mountain Farm

Born on a mountaintop, Sarah Josepha Hale always kept a clear eye on the horizon. As Sarah Buell she spent her childhood on a high mountaintop farm overlooking the Sugar River in Newport, New Hampshire. Each spring she watched eagerly for the rosy buds of the maples and the new green of birch trees to emerge from the dark, pointed firs below. Then sparkling brooks ran down into the valleys, and she heard cowbells announce the coming of the evening star and watched the night stars shine serenely over the dark mountain's curve.

She was fortunate in having a mother who loved learning and good books, a father who could tell her true stories of Indian raids and battle heroes, and a brother, only a year older, to share his books and his dreams with her.

In 1798, when Sarah was ten years old, there was no brightly painted school bus to take her, her brother Horatio, and younger sister Martha to school. Few schools existed in the "back country" at that time, and they could not have given the Buell children as good an education as they received at home from their mother. She told them stories from the Bible, read aloud from *Pilgrim's Progress* and from the poems of Robert Burns and William Shakespeare. She taught them the old English and Scottish ballads that were a part of their heritage. "She possessed a mind clear as rock water," Sarah wrote.

Sarah's mother was born Martha Whittlesey, of the Whittlesey family that settled in or near Saybrook, Connecticut, in the early 1630s. The men were literate and courageous, and they served their colony and country responsibly in both military and political posts. Bibles, sermons, and almanacs were handed down, along with records of the family history. A sense of posterity and a respect for books came with these ancient volumes.

Helping her mother to keep house, taking care of her sister Martha, learning to cook, sew, and knit left scant time for daydreaming, but Sarah had some private daydreams, nonetheless. When she could, she took her work or her book out-of-doors. She loved to lean against one of the tall pines that covered part of her mountain. The wind in the top branches sounded like the sea, her brother said. Her eldest brother Charles had been to sea. Sarah had only been as far from home as the village of Newport, under the mountain; but she could imagine a tall ship with a pine mast, cut perhaps from this very mountain, and how it might sway but never break in the stiff gales at sea. Before the war of the Revolution such tall pines had been reserved for the masts of the king's navy. Sarah felt close to those turbulent days, for her own father still suffered from wounds received in that war. She would never forget the stories he told or the sufferings of those soldiers on their long marches. Thus "the love of country was deeply engraved on my heart," she later wrote.

To do something for her country was one dream Sarah cherished. Another was to study, to learn all she could; although girls at that time were not given much encouragement in this. The place for women was in the home, and any female (a word Sarah came to despise) who hoped for something different was told that it would be unseemly.

Books, too, were scarce in those early times, and for

readers like Sarah and Horatio, who was preparing to enter Dartmouth College, they were priceless and sought out wherever they could be found. Sarah herself said later, "The books to which I had access were few, very few . . . but they were such as required to be studied, and I did study them. Next to the Bible and *Pilgrim's Progress*, my earliest reading was Milton, Johnson, Pope, Cowper, and a part of Shakespeare. . . ."

When only ten years old, Sarah read Nathaniel Ramsay's *History of the American Revolution*, not a book written for children. Every word about Gen. Horatio Gates's campaigns held special meaning, because her own father had served under Gates. George Washington was, of course, the hero, whose sudden death in 1799 was mourned by the whole nation. Though the new national capital was to be named after Washington, the inauguration of Thomas Jefferson as president, on March 4, 1801, marked a new era. Jefferson's hope for free public education would come nearer to fulfillment in Sarah's lifetime. And she was to aid its progress on behalf of women.

One day Sarah Buell discovered a book bearing the name of a woman—Ann Radcliffe—on its title page. (Most women in the 1800s published their works under men's names. The novelist George Eliot, for example, was an Englishwoman named Mary Ann Evans. Many books and articles were signed simply "By a Lady.") The first novel Sarah had ever read, this was called *The Mysteries of Udolpho*. Ann Radcliffe wrote what were later to be called Gothic novels. They were usually set against a background of haunted castles, where the heroine was imprisoned or went through harrowing adventures. Few of the books Sarah had known before had been written by Americans—and none by women. "But here was a work, the most fascinating I had ever read, always excepting *Pilgrim's Progress*, written by a woman! How happy it made me!"

No doubt *The Mysteries of Udolpho* was refreshing after

her struggle to keep up with Race (Horatio's nickname) in Latin and natural philosophy. Fortunately, Race was as eager to help her as Sarah was to learn.

"You must have Latin," he told her. "Mother says it is one of the roots of our language, and it is required for college." College! Sarah felt numb at that word. As far as she knew, no colleges admitted girls. And if they did, how would she find the money to go? Sewing, dressmaking, or millinery were the only respectable vocations for young ladies. Even for teaching school, men were chosen most often.

College meant something more. It meant that Race would be gone most of the year. She would miss his encouragement and his cheerful ways.

But at last, one September day, the Buell family gathered in the dooryard to see Race off to Dartmouth College in Hanover, fifty miles away. "Lectures will commence on September 25th next," the announcement read. It was a proud moment for the family, but mixed with sadness, for Gordon Buell, their father, was finding it increasingly difficult to carry on the farm without his sons. (Charles, his first-born, had been lost at sea.)

"We'll be looking for you at Thanksgiving. God be with you!" they called after Horatio. He turned to call and wave good-bye, and his thoughts lingered with them for awhile, especially with Sarah. He knew she did not begrudge him his opportunity. All the family had worked toward this goal for him, and Sarah would never stop trying to add to her store of learning. She had told him she would work on alone at Latin and mathematics and natural philosophy (which we now call "science"). He would write to her about all the new things he would be studying at Dartmouth.

2
A New Home and a Wedding

Sarah's parents had to think of a better way to make a living. Her father, easily tired and still feeling the pain in his old wound, was in favor of moving into the town of Newport to open an inn. He had already named it, optimistically, The Rising Sun.

Travelers passing through Newport could rest there on their way to and from Hanover and cities to the south. Mr. Buell, as innkeeper, hoped to make a better living for his family, with less hard work than farming required.

Sarah was sorry to leave East Mountain, but life would surely be easier for her parents in Newport. Mrs. Buell recognized, too, that her daughters needed the advantages of a town—even a small town. There would be a lending library, a sewing circle, church and community events, and new people to meet.

Newport was the gathering place for the farmers from the surrounding country, a cattle market at certain times of year, and a crossroads for stage coaches between Boston and Claremont, or Boston and Hanover. A French journalist (de Warville) wrote, ''Through all the United States a tavern-keeper must be a respectable man, his daughters are well-dressed, and have an air of decency and civility.'' He might have been speaking of Gordon Buell.

Also, in Newport Sarah could earn something by teaching school. Though even men teachers earned little, Sarah was excited and pleased when this idea was discussed. She had been writing down her thoughts and simple verses to amuse the younger children. And she could tell her pupils those stirring tales of the Revolution that she knew so well. The children should all know what their grandfathers and uncles had fought for at Saratoga and Bennington and Bunker Hill. Many of those who had fought at Bunker Hill were from New Hampshire.

In the long college vacations Race tutored his sister, so that—unlike most young women of her time—Sarah acquired an education almost equal to that of a college graduate. She was well qualified for her duties as a schoolmistress.

She eventually did teach in the little village of Guild, just east of Newport. Perhaps there she first noticed the lamb in the schoolyard and wrote her most famous poem, "Mary's Lamb." About this time she also wrote for the children "If ever I see—on bush or tree" and "Snow."

The kind of school Sarah kept was different from the old-fashioned "dame school," in which everything was learned by rote. Sarah saw to it that both boys *and* girls learned to read and to write, to do sums, and even to study Latin.

When The Rising Sun inn opened in 1810, in a large white clapboard building near Newport's village green, Race had graduated from Dartmouth and Sarah was twenty-one, a self-confident young lady, with a trim figure, neatly dressed. If she felt wanting in social poise, it was not apparent to anyone.

One day The Rising Sun welcomed a traveler, who decided to stay in Newport, held by the clear gaze of Sarah's hazel eyes. Young David Hale came from Alstead and Keene, New Hampshire, where he had studied law. His family included men prominent in scholarship and in government. Now David decided to "hang out his shingle," as the saying went, in Newport. He had a gift for making friends and a love of books and learning. He was a few years older than Sarah, but they had mutual interests, and Horatio Buell had begun to practice law, too—in Glens Falls, New York. Sarah's courtship hours with David were spent riding through the beautiful country, over the covered bridges, or walking beside the meandering Sugar River. Sarah later addressed a poem to the Sugar River:

Oh! may my verse, thy strength and beauty stealing,
    Flow like thy waters, and thy fame extend!
Thou minglest with the tide of life's young feeling—
    With thee my earliest recollections blend . . .

But sadness came before joy, for Sarah's mother did not live to see her daughter's wedding. On November 25, 1811, illness struck, and both Martha Buell and her younger daughter, only eighteen years old, died on the same day. The mother, the keystone of the Buell family, was gone. It was a double blow, and Sarah somehow had to find the courage and strength to continue teaching. Without the mother's guidance and encouragement The Rising Sun inn had to close.

At length, David persuaded Sarah not to postpone their wedding any longer, and on October 23, 1813, it took place at the former inn. Sarah described a wedding probably much like her own, in her novel: "It took place in the large hall of the town. All were arrayed in their best; the young ladies in white, the married in silks or crapes, the men mostly in suits of dark-coloured cloth." Near the middle of the hall the minister presided.

A wood fire blazed brightly in the ample chimney, and a number of candles and lamps were disposed   around   the   apartment. . . . The bridegroom entered leading by the hand a very amiable-looking girl with downcast eye and blushing cheek. She had one attendant of extraordinary beauty. The timidity of the trembling bride (who is the reverse of the groom in coloring), was remarked by all. She was a small, slender, delicate girl, and the wreath of white roses entwined amidst her fair hair was hardly paler than her cheek. Her dress was a frock of plain white muslin, trimmed around the bosom and sleeves with lace; the only ornament she wore was a gold chain around her neck, to which was attached a small miniature picture of a brother who had been drowned.

After a short pause, [the minister] inquired if they were ready to proceed; and on [David's] replying they were, he arose and all obeyed his motion. He made a short, but solemn prayer, fervently imploring a blessing on the couple; then addressing himself first to the bridegroom and then to the bride, he recapitulated in a pertinent and impressive manner, the duties which the marriage covenant imposed, and asked if they promised to perform them. A bow and courtesy answered in the affirmative—*no vocal response is necessary*—and he pronounced them 'lawfully married, etc.' and the ceremonies, the whole occupying fifteen or twenty minutes, were concluded.

Then followed a deep silence broken first by the Reverend Mr. _____ who addressed some advice to the young married pair, after which attendants brought in waiters [trays] filled with tumblers and glasses containing wine (the real juice of the grape) and cake—several kinds. The wedding cake was iced, and covered with sugar plums of all colors and forms, and tastefully decorated with myrtle and evergreen.

Of this cake all the young ladies, and by their persuasions, nearly all the young men, preserved a small slice to place beneath their pillows before retiring, it being the popular opinion that they should then be favored with dreams revealing their future.

This description was written by one who was to become an authority on manners, marriage, and, to some degree, fashion—over a period of fifty years. It shows how Sarah saw herself and contains the memory of that brother Charles who was lost at sea and whom she never forgot.

Sarah's husband—much like her brother Horatio—was patient and encouraged her desire for learning and literary pursuits. Their children always remembered their parents reading beside the lamplit table in the evenings. Sarah and David spent at least two hours each evening studying and always read some part of the Bible before retiring for the night. Among the poems Sarah wrote for her children, "Good Night," one of her best, conveys the sense of peace she cherished for her household:

> Good night, Good night, and peace be with you—
> Peace, that gentlest parting strain,
> Soft it falls like dew on blossoms,
> Cherishing within our bosoms,
> > Kind desires to meet again.
> > Good night, good night.
>
> . . .
>
> Good night, Good night, Oh, softly breathe it!
> 'Tis a prayer for those we love;
> Peace to-night and joy to-morrow

For our God, who shields the sparrow,
Hears us in his courts above.
Good night, good night.

Sarah managed her household well. The Hale children enjoyed skating and sleighing in winter and summer excursions for berry-picking, picnics beside the river, wildflower gathering—simple pleasures that Sarah felt induced "serenity of mind."

And it did seem that they would "live happily ever after," as the fairy tales said, until one September night in 1822 when David Hale took a sudden chill, which turned into pneumonia. Tragedy struck at Sarah in the worst possible way, for her loving husband died, leaving her with four children, all under eight years of age. Her fifth child, William, was born two weeks after his father's death. Along with grief came the realization that the income remaining from a country lawyer's fees was not enough to provide for his family after his death. "We had lived in comfort, but I was left poor," Sarah wrote.

While still sore with grief, she had to turn her thoughts to ways of earning a living. The second son, Horatio, was sent to Glens Falls, New York, to live with his uncle. Kind friends, including those of David Hale's Masonic lodge, helped, and as a temporary measure Sarah became a partner with her sister-in-law Hannah in a small millinery business. They even placed some advertisements in the local newspaper:

LADIES' MILLINERY

Brown cambrick, figured gauze, silk and mourning bonnets, caps and headdresses of the latest and most approved patterns kept constantly on hand. Feathers, rugs and towcloth received in payment for goods.

Mrs. and Miss Hale

However, there was competition. A Miss Pierce also advertised in the same newspaper that she had just returned from Boston . . . "with the latest London, Philadelphia, and Boston fashions for Ladies' dresses, and keeps for sale an assortment of *Bonnets and Caps*, etc."

Sarah Hale, with her active, searching intelligence, could not have found this either a satisfying or sufficient means of making a living. She had evidently decided not to remarry, which was the easiest road to take for most women of her time. She continued to write, both poetry and prose, and, like countless other literary-minded women, sent her work to the magazines, newspapers, and annuals in New Hampshire and Boston. It speaks well for the quality of her work that it emerged—from the thousands of poems that deluged the editors—and was published.

On January 31, 1826, a prize of twenty dollars was offered by the editors of the Boston *Spectator* and the *Ladies' Album* for the best-written poem on Charity. The award went to Sarah Josepha Hale, "well known as the author of *The Genius of Oblivion* and as the writer of much valuable poetry for the periodicals under the signature of 'Cornelia.' " *The Genius of Oblivion* was a small volume of Sarah's poems published in 1823 with the help of the Freemasons of New Hampshire.

Her husband had encouraged her to write and had helped her to improve her style. She knew him to be "a thorough scholar in the English classics and language." He had not underrated her intelligence because she was a woman. He would want her to continue such pursuits.

By 1827 she had finished a book-length manuscript, a novel entitled *Northwood*. This she sent to the Boston publishers, Bowles and Dearborn. It was accepted and published that same year, raising her hopes that writing could become a permanent source of income. *Northwood* was one of the first books to show the contrasting life-styles in the North and the South of the United States. *Uncle Tom's Cabin*, by Harriet Beecher Stowe, with its view of Negro slavery, did not appear until 1852. *Northwood* was a success and was also printed in England, where readers were charmed by its true, firsthand picture of American life, so different from what they had imagined.

Far in advance of the idea of an Atlantic alliance, Sarah Hale pointed out in *Northwood* the advantages to England of close ties with the United States.

In 1928 a critic of nineteenth-century literature wrote of *Northwood*, published in England as *Sidney Romalee: A New England Tale*:

> From the first the book was a best seller. England published it as *A New England Tale*. Though not so speedy in action as modern readers might demand . . . *Northwood* is still a fascinatingly readable book. Written when first Abolition was beginning to arouse sectional feeling, its locale sways from a Yankee farm to a Charleston plantation. The story itself is negligible compared with the vivid and authentic descriptions of contemporary life in both places. . . . In the style of novels of that time, the author's propaganda crops out boldly at the last: she suggests as a solution of the slavery problem that the forty thousand churches of America contribute each five dollars for the purpose of "educating and colonizing free people of color and emancipated slaves"—the Liberia idea.

Amid the congratulations and smiles of approval, Sarah often wished that her parents and her husband could have witnessed this proof of their confidence in her. Capt. Gordon Buell, her father, had died in 1819.

Like her own mother, Sarah was determined to give her children the best education to be had, no matter how hard she must work for it. Such purpose gave her the courage to pursue her career. To her readers she stated her objective frankly, to provide for and to educate her children. "What good are riches," she asked, "except to benefit those we love?"

3

Sarah in Boston

Only a month after the publication of *Northwood*, Sarah Josepha Hale received a letter from a Boston publisher, the Reverend John Lauris Blake, asking her if she would like to edit a new monthly magazine exclusively for women. What would she like better? Even when good friends advised against it, Sarah could not reject the idea. The *Ladies' Magazine*, as it was called, was to be the forerunner of many designed to give women the special kind of help and encouragement they needed.

In 1828 a magazine published exclusively for women and edited by a woman was a daringly new idea, although a few women were gaining a little recognition, after tremendous, lonely effort: women like Mary Lyon, who, after many years of struggle, founded Mount Holyoke Seminary, later to become Mount Holyoke College; and a certain pioneering educator named Emma Willard, who published *The Republic of America*, the first American history textbook written by a woman, which was praised by teachers as well as by the Marquis de Lafayette and Daniel Webster. In her Female Seminary at Troy, New York, Emma Willard offered science courses more advanced even than those available at some colleges for men. She was for many years a friend of Sarah Hale.

Sarah was forty or near it when the new career opened, but she did not look it. Always neat and fastidious in her dress and person, Sarah retained youthful good looks and a dainty bearing for most of her life. The painting by W. B. Chambers, made when she was sixty–two, shows a woman who could be twenty years younger. Although she wore black in mourning for her husband, there were always touches of white lace or a white collar. The black fabric could have been alpaca or silk. Silk was preferred because "it shook the dust," an advantage in those days of long dresses and unpaved streets. Sarah walked briskly and managed the full, sweeping skirts with ease.

Accepting the editorship meant that she would have to leave her New Hampshire hills and move to Boston. It would require all her courage—a widow with five children—but Sarah recognized it immediately as a call to which she could give only one answer. She quoted on her first editorial page:

> Our doubts are traitors
> And make us lose the good we oft might win
> By fearing to attempt.

For the upbringing of her children, too, Sarah held her hopes high. There were good schools in Boston, and she even aimed to educate her boys at Harvard College.

Because of her previous correspondence with editors of Boston periodicals and publishing houses, Sarah thought she might make congenial acquaintances and would feel at home in Boston. The city was then not only the commercial capital of New England but was rapidly becoming a center for writers, editors, and publishers. It was the home of the scholarly *North American Review* and many learned societies such as the American Academy of Arts and Sciences, the American Antiquarian Society, and the Boston Athenaeum.

The Hales lived in modest lodgings—probably a boarding-house—at first, but Sarah enjoyed introducing her children to Boston's famous sites, with the aid of Caleb Snow's *History of Boston*. On the famous Common, Lafayette, one of her heroes, had recently dined in a marquee with twelve hundred people, after laying the foundation stone of the Bunker Hill Monument. In Boston, eloquence in the persons of Edward Everett and William Ellery Channing held large congregations spellbound. And to Boston came Francis Parkman, the historian, and poets John Greenleaf Whittier and Henry Wadsworth Longfellow, to consult their publishers.

It was Boston at its most beautiful. The architect, Charles Bulfinch, had recently completed many handsome residences, a fine new state house with a gold-leaf dome, a rebuilt Faneuil Hall, and several churches. These beautiful structures, with Boston's overarching elms and green-shaded lanes, were to give the city its tone of dignity and serenity for decades to come.

All the auspices were favorable for Sarah Josepha Hale as she set vigorously to work. "My first object was to promote the education of my own sex," she wrote. She worked hard month after month, contributing herself nearly half of the poetry, fiction, and articles in the *Ladies' Magazine*.

The "adventure promised advantages in educating my children—and I accepted," said Sarah about her decision to go to Boston. Among the educational advantages in Boston at this time were the classes in music given in the Bowdoin Street church under Lowell Mason. Here children were taught free, and a series of public concerts was given in 1832–1833 to demonstrate the success of his teaching. The concerts delighted the audiences, and the Boston Academy of Music was founded to promote musical education in communities.

Lowell Mason read Sarah Hale's poems and urged her to collect them in a volume called *Poems for Our Children*, which was published in 1830. She also wrote the verses for many of Dr. Mason's very successful school music books. They were unique at the time and were used throughout the country. In *Juvenile Lyre, or Hymns and Songs, Religious, Moral and Cheerful for the use of Primary and Common Schools*, he included Sarah's "If ever I see" and "Mary's Lamb." The latter achieved such wide circulation and popularity that it is still included in many "Mother Goose" books!

Boston was also the publishing center for a good many of the annuals or gift books that decorated the parlor tables of the day. With titles such as *The Ladies' Wreath, The Snow Flake, The Christian Souvenir,* and *The Crocus,* bound in leather or silk and velvet, the annuals catered to the country's desire for "culture." The annual was the forerunner of what is called today the "coffee-table book," a large, handsome, expensively illustrated book, given or purchased for status reasons. In Boston the principal publisher of such books was Samuel G. Goodrich. Sarah Hale contributed stories or poems to a number of his annuals and edited others. They gave authors, especially women, an outlet for their talents and also contributed to the success of American artists. Poems by Edgar Allan Poe and Oliver Wendell Holmes were published in the annuals, although Holmes spoke disparagingly of seeing his "literary bantlings swathed in green silk and reposing in the drawing room."

Sarah Hale became associated with Samuel Goodrich in another way. He had introduced a series of books for children called *Tales of Peter Parley.* He did not sign them because, he said, "I hesitated to believe that I was qualified to appear before the public as an author, and in the next place, nursery literature had not then acquired the respect in the eyes of the world it now enjoys." He told no one but his wife and one of his sisters of his authorship, yet it was discovered and first divulged "by a woman—Mrs. Sarah J. Hale, to whom by the way I am indebted for many kind offices in my literary career."

Doubtless Mr. Goodrich was helpful to her in introducing her to potential contributors to her new magazine. It was a great challenge to gather articles, poems, and other writings for a magazine designed exclusively for women for she knew that "no publication of the kind had been long sustained." She depended upon introductions to eminent booksellers and publishers, such as Goodrich and William Ticknor, who knew many writers, and on her own wide reading and literary judgment.

The Reverend John Lauris Blake, who had invited her to take charge, was also a source of help for, though Sarah had a strong background in literature, she lacked practical experience in running a magazine. How must texts be prepared to go to the printer? With what printers should she deal? How and when could corrections be made? All these and more were questions that Sarah had to raise. She must have had many conferences with John Blake, whose interests and upbringing were so much like her own.

Blake had been a New Hampshire farmer's son, born in Northwood—which Sarah had chosen for the title of her first book. He had studied for the ministry at Phillips Academy in Exeter, New Hampshire, and in 1820 had established a successful school for young ladies in Concord. Eighty pupils from six different states attended it, and "there was no school at the time of higher reputation." He shared, then, Sarah's concern for the education of women. His interest in children had led him to try to improve their textbooks. By 1828 he had written a geography that suggested new and better methods of instruction, which were later adopted by others. He had published the *Biblical Reader*, and the *Historical Reader*, among other books.

With his wife and their two sons, Henry and Alexander, he had moved to Boston, intending to open a school there like the one he had had in Concord. But competition was tougher in Boston, and Mr. Blake became more deeply involved in writing and editing. He and his wife were prepared to give Sarah Hale every assistance in her new career.

William Ticknor, the bookseller-publisher, was also born on a New Hampshire farm. He, too, had come to Boston in search of success, and because he loved books. And in the 1830s he was well on his way to achieving a high standing as a publisher of the works of popular authors, both English and American. Most unusual, he insisted upon paying for publishing the works of English authors at a time when many United States publishers were taking full advantage of the lack of a copyright law to pirate editions of Dickens, Scott, and other best-selling British writers.

Ticknor's bookstore, at the corner of Washington and School streets in Boston, became a gathering place for many bookish Bostonians who were eager to glimpse or rub elbows with such favorite authors as Longfellow or Hawthorne. The store was familiarly called the "Old Corner," the word "bookstore" scarcely needing to be added. It also carried various items useful to writers, such as stationery and pens. An early fountain pen, which Sarah Hale may have tried, was "Livett & Parker's Improved Writing Instrument, combining Pen, Ink, and Ever-Point Pencil." This pen was advertised as containing a supply of ink sufficient for several days' use.

Near the "Old Corner" was Haven's Coffee-room, where Ticknor's writers and customers sought refreshment. Sarah Hale surely tasted Mrs. Haven's famous thick lemon pie, or "jumbles," or cream cakes. One can imagine her there relaxing and chatting with a friend across one of the marble-topped tables.

Sarah Hale lived for a time in the same lodging house as Oliver Wendell Holmes, who was then attending Harvard Medical School and occasionally writing poetry. Since he sat at the same boardinghouse table with Sarah, possibly one of the breakfast companions in his book *The Autocrat of the Breakfast Table* was modeled on Sarah. Could she have been "the Model of All the Virtues" or "the School Mistress" or "the lady in black bombazine"? Sarah Hale and young Holmes became friends—and corresponded after she had moved away. He sent her one of the rare autographed copies of this book. "The persistent editor," he called her, as he often had to refuse her requests for verse. He did not consider himself "one of the regular army of literateurs," he said. His poem "The Chambered Nautilus," written much later, always remained one of her favorites.

Sarah Hale had the vision to realize that an *American* literature *would* come into being, although there was little evidence of it as yet. "The work will be national—be American," she promised in her first editorial for the *Ladies' Magazine.* She wished to encourage American writers and was one of the few to review the first book of poems by Edgar Allan Poe. "A part are exceedingly boyish, feeble, and altogether deficient in the common characteristics of poetry; but . . . parts too of considerable length . . . remind us of no less a poet than Shelley. The author, who appears to be very young, is evidently a fine genius, but he wants judgment, experience, tact."

Later she published Poe's story "The Oblong Box," his "Marginal Notes," and the controversial "Literati." Her part in promoting and publishing the work of American writers was important at a time when all "refinements"—most people thought—had to come out of England or from abroad, and so mirrored English life and thought rather than American. Holmes remarked that American children were forced to read of larks and nightingales instead of yellowbirds and bobolinks, and were confused by pictures of the robin as a "little domestic bird that fed at table instead of a great, fidgety, jerky, whooping thrush." Sarah Hale believed that American literature, with its own flora and fauna, its own flavor and style, was germinating, and she wished to encourage it. Soon after she became editor the word *American* was prefixed to the title of the *Ladies' Magazine*.

Meanwhile, Sarah's own children were growing up and the expenses of their education were increasing. David, the oldest boy, became a cadet at the U.S. Military Academy at West Point. His brother Horatio registered at Harvard College in July 1829. It all meant longer working hours for their mother, who supplemented her editorial salary by more writing and compiling of books. She contributed to and edited certain issues of the children's magazine, *Juvenile Miscellany*, otherwise edited by Lydia Maria Child.

To complete her children's education was her acknowledged goal in life. She grasped every oppotunity to add to her income and the sale of her books. Yet she still had time and energy for many good works.

4

Help for the Shipwrecked

Among the unique personalities in Boston were Father Taylor, the Sailor's Preacher, and his wife, the former Deborah Millet of Marblehead. Edward T. Taylor had led a seafaring life himself before he married and settled down in Boston. He had wandered from port to port, always staying close to the seamen whom he best understood and who understood him. He had preached in kitchens and schoolhouses and on ships about to leave on long whaling voyages, and his sermons were salted with the vivid language and lore of the sea. His fame spread far and wide, not only among sailors. Of all the famous preachers in Boston at the time, Father Taylor was the one sought out by Charles Dickens on his visit in 1843. Dickens wrote:

> The only preacher I heard in Boston was Mr. Taylor . . . I found his chapel down among the shipping in one of the narrow, old, water-side streets, with a gay blue flag waving freely from its roof. . . . The preacher already sat in the pulpit, which was raised on pillars, and ornamented behind him with painted drapery of a lively and somewhat theatrical appearance. He looked a weather-beaten hard-featured man, of about six or eight-and-fifty;

with deep lines graven as it were into his face, dark hair, and a stern, keen eye. Yet the general character of his countenance was pleasant and agreeable.

The service commenced with a hymn, to which succeeded an extemporary prayer. . . . That done he opened his discourse. . . . He handled his text in all kinds of ways, and twisted it into all manner of shapes; but always ingeniously, and with a rude eloquence, well adapted to the comprehension of his hearers. . . . His imagery was all drawn from the sea, and from the incidents of a seaman's life; and was often remarkably good. He spoke to them of "that glorious man, Lord Nelson," and of Collingwood. . . . Sometimes, when much excited with his subject, he had an odd way—compounded of John Bunyan and Balfour of Burley—of taking his great quarto bible under his arm in the manner I have described, and pursued his discourse after this manner:

"Who are these—who are they—who are these fellows? Where do they come from? Where are they going to?—Come from! What's the answer?" —leaning out of the pulpit, and pointing downward with his right hand: "From below!"—starting back again, and looking at the sailors before him: "From below, my brethren. From under the hatches of sin, battened down above you by the evil one." . . . A walk up and down the pulpit: "And where are you going?"—stopping abruptly: "Aloft!"—very softly, and pointing upward: "Aloft!"—louder: "aloft!" —Louder still: "That's where you are going—with a fair wind—all taut and trim, steering direct for Heaven in its glory, where there are no storms or foul weather, and where the wicked cease from troubling, and the weary are at rest. . . . It's a

blessed harbour—still water there, in all changes of
the winds and tides; no driving ashore upon the
rocks, or slipping your cables and running out to
sea there: Peace—Peace—Peace—all peace!"
Another walk, and patting the bible under his left
arm: "What! These fellows are coming from the
wilderness, are they? From the dreary, blighted
wilderness of Iniquity, whose only crop is Death.
But do they lean upon anything?—do they lean
upon nothing, these poor seamen?" Three raps
upon the bible: "Oh, yes. Yes. They lean upon the
arm of their Beloved."—three more raps: "upon the
arm of their Beloved"—three more, and a walk:
"Pilot, guiding-star, and compass, all in one, to all
hands—here it is. . . . They can come, even these
poor fellows can come, from the wilderness leaning
on the arm of their Beloved, and go up—up—up!"
raising his hand higher, and higher, at every
repetition of the word, so that he stood with it at
last stretched above his head, regarding them in a
strange, rapt manner, and pressing the book
triumphantly to his breast, until he gradually
subsided into some other portion of his discourse.

Walt Whitman, too, sought out Father Taylor. He wrote:

I have never heard but one essentially perfect
orator. In the spring or autumn, quiet Sunday
forenoons, I liked to go down early to the quaint
ship-cabin-looking church where the old man
minister'd—to enter and leisurely scan the building,
the low ceiling . . . smell the aroma of old
wood—to watch the auditors, sailors, mates,
"matlows," officers, singly or in groups as they
came in—their physiognomies, forms, dress, gait

> . . . seating themselves in the rude, roomy, un-
> door'd, uncushioned pews and the evident effect
> upon them of the place, occasion, and atmos-
> phere . . .

Sailors heading into Boston looked forward as much to hearing one of Father Taylor's sermons as to sighting the gilded grasshopper weather vane on old Faneuil Hall; both were familiar landmarks.

In the 1830s a record number—almost 1,500—sailing ships tied up at Boston docks. The memory of her seafaring brother Charles perhaps drew Sarah to North Square where the seamen's chapel was and eventually to join with Deborah Taylor in helping the shipwrecked wives and families of the sailors. She saw poverty on the streets of Boston, want and hunger on the faces of children and their mothers. How could she help them?

However it came about, she soon became active in forming the Seaman's Aid Society. Understanding the plight of widows, she wrote, "many of these have once lived in comfort, some even in affluence—but the destroyer came; and in one day their homes and hearts were left desolate, and sorrow and poverty were their only earthly inheritance." Her own hearth had been desolated by the "grim destroyer."

Sarah pleaded for the victims. The sailor "may have assisted in the transfer of riches of every quarter of the globe—but none of the treasure belonged to him. Through his agency the prosperity of our country may have been abundantly increased—but his lot was still labor, peril and poverty. The nature of his calling renders it almost certain that his widow and orphans will be left destitute."

With other Boston women, Sarah and Deborah Taylor began by making simple, sturdy clothes for these poor, bereaved ones. Soon they realized that what these people needed was not charity but employment. They must be given the means to work and to sew for themselves and for the sailors, and they must be paid at fair rates for their work. Most seamen then had to buy poorly made garments from the "slop shops" at high prices. "Slop shops" was the term for stores selling cheap ready-made clothing and other articles used by sailors.

Before long the Seaman's Aid Society was not only giving needlework instruction to the wives and children but providing the sailors themselves with well-made clothing that would hold together and keep them warm during the rough work and weather they had to endure. Sound reasoning went into the project and many uncounted hours of devoted work. In a year or two the Seamen's Aid Society's "work basket expanded into a well-supplied Clothing Store," where "we have received upwards of $5,000 for garments sold, chiefly to seamen," Sarah reported.

The three ways in which a poor woman might make a living for herself and her children, Sarah wrote, were "domestic service, washing, and needlework." Sarah called public attention to the need for education and the means to self-help for the poor. The object of the Seaman's Aid Society was "to cooperate with the Boston Port Society in the effort to improve the condition and character of Seamen and their families."

Soon a Sabbath and Infant School was established. Daughters of seamen were taught "plain needlework in addition to the common branches of instruction." In every meeting with other volunteers, Sarah Hale emphatically stated that the learning of needlework was an "absolute necessity" to these girls. She urged that the public schools of Boston include it in the curriculum. During 1836 the Society's school taught between thirty and forty young girls the common branches of an English education in the forenoon, while afternoons were devoted to "needlework and oral instruction in the social, moral and religious duties of females." The school was held in a neat apartment under the Seamen's Bethel in North Square, Boston. Sarah realized that the school would have a deeper influence and provide more lasting aid than mere almsgiving.

In its first year a library was added. Known as The Seaman's Society Library, it was "free for the Seamen of Boston and their families, and likewise for all Seamen while in this city." Through donations, including some from "our liberal Boston booksellers," nearly three hundred books were put on the shelves the first year. The society now provided "a well-warmed reading room, furnished with daily papers, and useful and entertaining books." This was the first such library for seamen, and the forerunner of all seamen's libraries that opened in cities all over the world.

Giving a "just price" for the wives' labor resulted in friction with the "slop shops," which paid only enough to keep the women in grinding poverty, while cheating the sailors by providing inferior goods.

The seamen's boardinghouses were another source of corruption. They were badly managed, ill-kept, and the men there were exposed to rum—the scourge of the poor. Sarah Hale and her group of women were determined to give these houses stiff and healthy competition.

Sarah was not timid in identifying and exposing the evils that beset the common sailor and his family. In 1837 she stated, "the present boarding-house system must be swept away, like an unclean thing, before much real, permanent improvement can be effected. And since our last Report one suggestion then made has been acted upon—the 'Seaman's Home' has been provided." The ladies were urged to contribute their unused furniture to make this house comfortable for the seamen—a house that, like a "pleasant island," would benefit from the "soft breezes of the morning diffusing life, health and happiness."

Rent gougers, too, must be discouraged. Seamen's wives,

widows, and the men themselves were at the mercy of ruthless, greedy landlords, who obliged a poor woman to pay for two rooms when she needed only one, in order to get the one, and "by this extortion" added "a few more dollars to his store." The Seamen's Home would help to set a standard and a guideline by charging only a reasonable rent. Naturally, smart sailors would patronize the home and help to put the rent gougers out of business. Or so she and her colleagues hoped. Low-rent housing, Sarah wrote, should be provided by the benevolent who, instead of "adorning the city with splendid, palace-like dwellings for the wealthy," should consider forming an association "to build some neat, commodious comfortable houses, prepared purposely to accommodate those who are able to hire only one room." She even spoke of "the effect of environment on character," something that was not studied or acknowledged until the twentieth century.

Sarah pleaded eloquently, but the problem still exists.

Another, more delicate, subject, she dared to raise in her annual reports. "It is one which cannot be remedied without legislative interference; yet concerning so deeply . . . our sex, we think that ladies should take some cognizance of the matter. We allude to the law which gives to the husband uncontrolled power over the personal property of his wife. Though she possessed a million of dollars before she marries, she cannot, after she is a wife, dispose of a dollar in her own right." She went on to illustrate "the flagrant injustice of this law" in its operation on both rich and poor. "We cannot believe," she adds with her usual tactfulness, "that wise and good men, if they were once aroused to thought on this subject, would wish this law to remain as it now is. And although the fortunate ladies, who constitute the Seaman's Aid Society, may not one of them suffer in consequence of the statute; yet, they should feel nonetheless for those who are subjected to its demoralizing and soul-withering influence."

It is easy to see how Dickens—with his compassion for the poor, downtrodden, and exploited—was attracted to the Seamen's Bethel in Boston.

Following the unusually severe storms of 1839, the demands upon the Seamen's Home were great. "Orphan boys have fled to us, the gray-headed sailor, the colored sailor, and even officers, have come without shoes or jackets to put on, having lost all, and only escaped to tell their sufferings. Some have been sick, and some sorrowful, and we rejoiced that we had means to make them comfortable," wrote the superintendent.

"We do not attempt to count the cost of time and thought which has been given," Sarah wrote, "nor the patience, kindness, self-denials, and self-sacrifices which he who has had the personal responsibility of this establishment on his hands has had to feel and exercise. Such labors of love can only be known and rewarded by Him who seeth not as man seeth."

Sarah's own hours donated to the Seamen's Aid Society went on, uncounted too, until she moved to Philadelphia.

This effort to aid seamen and their families was the first in the United States. Similar societies, which afterwards sprang up in major seaports, owed their existence and inspiration to the one founded in Boston by Sarah J. Hale.

5

A Special Piece of Ground

Another major enterprise—apart from her editorial work—that won Sarah's devotion was the Bunker Hill Monument.

On one of her sightseeing trips she came upon a scene of desolation in Charlestown where the bloody battle of Bunker Hill had been fought in June of 1775. She was expecting to see a handsome memorial tablet or monument to the valiant dead, considering the elaborate ceremony held when the foundation stone was laid in 1825. Lafayette had come over from France and Daniel Webster looking "his very greatest" had delivered a ringing address, yet here on the site three years later was only a jagged, unfinished shaft, with other granite blocks almost as large scattered around on the ground. It looked like a disaster area or an abandoned quarry more than a monument to heroes.

Sarah's sense of the fitness of things was outraged. Something must be done! She soon learned that the monument, designed to rise to 221 feet, was stunted for lack of funds. She called attention to the need for action in the *Ladies' Magazine*.

The movement to build a monument had begun in April 1822, when the following notice appeared in the *Boston Patriot*:

BUNKER HILL

A lot of ground, including the monument erected to the memory of Gen. Warren, and the remains of the "Breast Work," thrown up on the eve of the Battle fought on that spot on the 17 of June 1775, is advertised to be sold at auction the first day of May.

As a site so memorable should not be covered with buildings, it is hoped that some patriotic gentlemen of wealth in the town of Charlestown will purchase this American Marathon and have it enclosed with a stone or iron fence, to be held sacred, as the spot where the defenders of the Republic first met the shock of battle "in times which tried men's souls."

No stranger from other States visits this part of the Union who does not wish to stand where fought the Champions of Liberty. Future generations will hold that blood-stained height in proud remembrance. There repose the ashes of the brave; there was planted the Tree of Liberty. Let not the glorious sepulchre of our Revolutionary warriors be profaned.

This appeal was written by General H. A. S. Dearborn, son of the Captain Henry Dearborn who had fought at Bunker Hill under Colonel John Stark. Soon after, several gentlemen contributed funds to buy the land for a monument to commemorate the battle. Dr. J. C. Warren of Boston purchased the acreage in November 1822 and held it until the Monument Association was formed and took title. Those who joined in these first efforts to salvage the site bore illustrious names: Honorable Daniel Webster, Professor George Ticknor, Dr. John C. Warren, nephew of Dr. Joseph

Warren, the patriot leader who fell in the battle. Others were the Honorable William Sullivan, the Honorable George Blake, and William Tudor, Esq., founder of both the Boston Athenaeum and the *North American Review.* They decided on the type of monument that should be erected and the Monument Association was incorporated.

Another committee of men of "high cultivation and taste" (Daniel Webster, Loammi Baldwin, George Ticknor, Gilbert Stuart, and Washington Allston—the last two artists of renown) voted that an obelisk should be erected and approved the design and plans of Solomon Willard. Willard agreed to serve as architect and superintendent of the work; at first he declined compensation but finally accepted $500 a year for expenses. He is said to have walked more than 300 miles to examine different quarries in order to locate the best stone and to find the best means for bringing it to the site undamaged. He steadily refused to take any profit from the work.

However, after the gala occasion of the laying of the foundation stone, the monument came to several embarrassing halts.

When it had reached nearly forty feet, in September 1828, the Monument Association was forced to borrow money on the security of the land; when the association was in debt for a total of $23,000, early in 1829, they were forced to call a halt to the work. Various efforts were made to raise funds. In January 1830, Sarah Hale proposed to "raise the requisite funds by an appeal to the ladies of New England," an offer that was gratefully acknowledged and accepted. In February Sarah suggested in the *Ladies' Magazine* that the 900,000 women of New England each give twenty-five cents to the cause of finishing Bunker Hill Monument. "This is a *second* appeal to our readers." Still the public response was inadequate.

Not everyone wanted the monument project to succeed.

Some said it was time to forget long-ago battles. Others felt that the women were too bold in pressing to get it completed. Sarah Hale could not "feel indifferent to the slightest word of censure." Writing to General Dearborn on February 24, 1830, she said, "As for the expectation that the ladies were to bear off the palm from the men, and raise the monument as a proof of female magnanimity, no such silly thought ever entered my heart, and if I were convinced the measure would increase the vanity . . . of my sex . . . I would oppose it with all the influence I possess." As to having her name on the monument, she would "as soon think of having it inscribed on the moon. I shall propose, and I hope all the ladies will agree with me, that not a single individual name appear in this transaction. I would not have a certificate or record of any kind remain to tell the world what the ladies have done."

In the summer of 1831, the Hon. Edward Everett, then a congressman and a most convincing public speaker, made a strong appeal that the land not be sold. Yet, after all this eloquence, very little action followed. Still, the eminent Boston merchant, Amos Lawrence, refused to give up the project and in September 1831 offered to subscribe $5,000, on condition that $50,000 should be raised within a year, to save the land and raise the obelisk. Only in extreme necessity should the land be sold, he felt, adding, "I should personally sooner vote to sell ten acres of the Common in front of my house to pay the city debt, than vote to sell the ten acres on Bunker Hill, until it shall appear that our citizens will not contribute the means of saving it." Mr. Lawrence continued his urgent offers and solicitations to influential people.

At a public meeting called by the Monument Association and held in Faneuil Hall on May 28, 1833, the Hon. Edward Everett again added his prestige and persuasion to the cause by addressing the large gathering. Through various efforts, including the Ladies' Fund, nearly $20,000 was collected, enough to resume the building. However, this amount fell short of what was needed, and at eighty feet the work was again halted.

Eventually, the association's only big asset, the ten acres of land, had to be sold. The original planners may have been plunged in gloom by now, but a solid few like Amos Lawrence still held to their plan: preservation of the site and a well-proportioned obelisk, not a stump, to honor the brave who had shed their blood for liberty. Mr. Lawrence doubled his offer early in 1839. "If the B.H.M.A. will collect $30,000 the present year and pay off the debt, I will give . . . $10,000 to enable it to complete the work in a manner that our fathers would have done, had they been here to direct it," he wrote. Another patriot and former Bostonian, Judah Touro, then living in New Orleans, donated $10,000 also. Despite these generous urgings, the Monument Association, in June 1840, must have had some confirmed pessimists on its board, for its annual report expressed grave doubt that the present generation would witness completion of the monument!

Here the women entered the scene. The men's doubts were "repeated within a few days in a sewing circle of Boston, and several ladies proposed the idea of a Fair in behalf of the object." Whose sewing circle? Clearly one chaired by Mrs. Sarah J. Hale, who, in 1830, ten years before, had proposed a similar project.

In the interim the men had put forth their best efforts—and failed, though some of them were still eager to push the work to completion.

The country was recovering from the depression of 1837–1838. People were becoming more aware of the importance of preserving the American heritage. A poem, "Old Ironsides," by young Oliver Wendell Holmes had aroused the public to a pitch that caused Congress to vote to restore the frigate *Constitution* instead of scrapping her. Sarah Hale, through her successful magazine and other charitable efforts, had proved herself to Boston civic leaders, and more attention was paid to her suggestions. Her *Ladies' Magazine* was building a nationwide circulation. Whatever the combination of reasons, a last-ditch effort was now mounted.

"The suggestion at once received favor" and before June ended the board of directors of the Monument Association formally sanctioned the idea of the fair and got behind it. Newspapers throughout New England carried the appeal. The women of New England, and indeed of the whole United States, were urged to make their contributions.

"Some editors are against us," Mrs. Hale admitted, "but the Ladies' Society is being organized." With her usual consideration for the male side of the family, she welcomed all but did not recommend that any woman "join without the consent of her immediate protector."

Ten socially prominent women comprised her committee of correspondence. Sarah was deliberately using the Revolutionary War term as most suitable to the occasion. And again she was venturing into new territory, for no magazine—certainly no women's magazine—in America had allied itself to a public program of this kind before.

Here was woman's opportunity, and Sarah's cohorts did not fail her. What did they have to offer? Their devotion, their persuasive and intellectual skills, their intelligence, their skill at needlework and other crafts, the sanctioned sphere of women. They would put them all to work for this good purpose.

It is hard for us to see how, in a day when nearly everything had to be done by hand (no typewriters, no telephones, no radio, no linotype machines), it was all accomplished—and in so short a time. A tremendous single-minded effort was put forth. It swept New England and other parts of the nation, giving proof of the remarkable publicizing and organizing ability of its prime mover, Sarah J. Hale.

A fair was to be held in Quincy Hall, Boston, in September of that same year, she announced, and it would continue for seven days, *"exclusively under the direction of the ladies,* although with the hearty cooperation and efficient aid of gentlemen who had, from the first, labored in behalf of the object." Every article donated to the fair would be sold for the benefit of the monument.

In addition to managing the fair, which meant countless hours of correspondence with towns and individuals all over the states, Mrs. Hale edited a special news bulletin, *The Monument.* This was distributed to those at the fair and used as promotion to those who were merely thinking of attending. Each issue of eight closely printed pages cited the noble purposes of the fair and the monument, and its educational value to children. It published letters of encouragement from old soldiers of the Revolution, columns of poetry, names of the towns that had tables at the fair. Ads described featured articles for sale, and there were daily progress reports on attendance and funds received.

Sarah Hale praised the efforts of the men who had arranged the decorations:

> As you enter the Rotunda, look upward to the light and graceful decorations from the roof —around on the bannered ceiling, and down the long vista, where, on either hand, are ranged the table of the ladies, and there before us is the beautiful and unique ornament of dahlias—and beneath, that which will attract more eyes and more hearts than all the decorations—the portrait of General Joseph Warren!
>
> . . . What good taste (alias, good sense) the

Committee of Gentlemen have shown in decorating
the Hall. All is simple, yet the effect is magnificent.

Colonel Prescott's sword, "the sword of a hero," was on
display, and a model of "The Monument, as it is to be."

While all due praise was given to the efforts of the ladies in
preparing articles for sale, arranging them, and attending the
tables, the men were invited to *buy*.

> We have millions of useful and substantial ar-
> ticles for the economical, thousands of pretty and
> elegant things for the fanciful, and a few costly and
> ornamental luxuries, which we hope the rich will
> purchase. Surely when the ladies have made such
> exertions the gentlemen will not fail to do their part.
> They hold the purse strings, and must be the
> patrons of the fair.

Generous donors from outside New England sent six
hundred dollars in cash and a group of women from
Brooklyn, New York, sent two cases of their own handwork.

On the second day, 12,000 people attended the fair. On
Friday, 8,000 door tickets were sold, "and as many
thousands of choice and useful things were sold from the
tables." On Friday, too, an ominous line appeared in *The
Monument*, preceded by a pointing finger. It read, "Look out
for pickpockets."

As the week went on, new items were added to the stock.
Autograph collectors found for sale, at one dollar each,
letters of members of the Burr family, of William Godwin, of
Mary Wollstonecraft, and the autographs of General
Washington, the Marquis de Lafayette, and James Madison.
The Medford table offered a painting by Van Dyke. A "new
and elegant article at Table No. 10" was a harp stand. A
Chickering piano was given by Mr. Chickering to be sold at

the fair. A delegation from Louisiana purchased for $200 the perfect replica of the monument, "as it is to be," which had adorned the center of the rotunda. "A noble proof of their sympathy with our object, as well as of their patriotism."

On Monday (the fair was not open on Sunday) the editor of *The Monument* launched the day on a confident note:

> We have so far succeeded in our purpose that we can confidently say—"it is accomplished": the requisite sum to complete the Bunker Hill Monument, $25,000, will be obtained by the close of tomorrow's evening. To that time we limit our Fair. All who wish to contribute to our funds, or see the decorations of the Hall . . . must come soon. . . . We have made arrangements to admit children at half price, and several schools free, and trust hundreds will avail themselves of the privilege. We hope parents and teachers will explain to the children under their care the object of the display in Quincy Hall. We think that there are few children in our land, but would feel a deep interest, were the subject rightly set before them, in contributing (by the purchase of some trifle at the Fair) to the completion of the Obelisk at Bunker Hill. The impression which this scene cannot but make on their little hearts, will never, in this life, be effaced. It may be the means of exciting them to emulate the examples of patriotism and goodness, which they will see are so highly respected. We shall watch and welcome their entrance, as we would spring flowers or April sun-shine.

The fair was a happy event—and a successful one, and if some of the details and plans for fund-raising seem familiar to us, they were new then. Such fairs, especially such an extended event managed entirely by women for a patriotic nonprofit purpose, were rare. Sarah J. Hale could look upon this, one of her last public achievements before leaving Boston, with considerable satisfaction.

With the proceeds from the fair, some $30,000, and the donations of Messrs. Lawrence and Touro of $10,000 each, together with over $5,000 from other sources, the monument was raised to its full height. Early on the morning of July 23, 1842, the "last stone was raised in presence of the Officers of the Association, the American flag being waved from it during its ascent and under a salute from the Charlestown Artillery."

Sarah J. Hale should have been standing near to watch this triumphant raising, but it is more likely that by then she was in Philadelphia—on editorial business. Then it was not possible to hop a plane to Boston to witness such an event. The journey of 350 miles would have taken several days.

6

A Gain and a Loss

Although Louis E. Godey has through the years been credited with inaugurating the use of colored fashion plates in American magazines, in the first issue of Sarah's magazine, published at the end of 1830, she promised her readers six plates in forthcoming issues—engravings or lithographs "the best our American artists can furnish." In 1833 four of these were tinted fashion plates. She also included much information on phrenology, the popular new "science," which was taking hold in Boston, and a page embossed with the alphabet and the Lord's Prayer "to give readers . . . an idea of the manner in which books are prepared for those who read with their fingers." This was certainly a unique way to call attention to the newly founded Boston Institution for the Blind. Music was also included in certain issues of the magazine.

Beginning in January 1834 Mrs. Hale announced that her magazine would be renamed *The American Ladies' Magazine*, since she had found that there was a British periodical called the *Ladies' Magazine*. She added: 'The march of decoration has now become quite an adjunct to the march of mind. Pictures and pretty covers are as essential to the success of a book, as scenery and spectacle to the success of the stage. We do not promise 'all sorts' of pictures and engravings; but those that are introduced will be in good taste." She also expressed pride in the number and quality of the contributors to the magazine. "We number among our contributors for the six years past almost all the distinguished literary ladies of our own country. Sigourney, Sedgwick, Gilman, Embury, Smith (authoress of "A Winter in Washington") Child, Gould, Wells, Willard, Phelps, Locke, and others. . . ." Pictures and pretty covers, however, added to the expenses, as indicated in her notice in the December issue:

TO OUR FRIENDS

The present number completes the seventh volume of the *American Ladies' Magazine.* Seven years—it seems a long time in prospects, but care and hope, anxiety and gratification lend an excitement to life, which causes the sands of time to flow rapidly away. The years have seemed short, for each *month* has had its task and its enjoyment.

When commencing the Magazine, I proposed, in my own mind, that, should it prove successful, and my health permit, I would conduct it for ten years—then I hoped the education of my children would be so far advanced as to render such incessant exertions on my part less necessary. My work, till the present year, has answered my expectations, and been better sustained by the public than any other literary Magazine in New England. But owing to the depression of business last winter, which deeply affected the bookselling trade, my list of subscribers was much diminished, and my profits, in consequence, are quite small. Still I am not discouraged. Business has revived, and I feel confident my friends will lend their assistance to raise my list again. I am aware there are a number of new periodicals soliciting public patronage, and deserving it too—but my work, devoted as it is to the mental, moral and religious improvement of my own sex, has claims which, I trust, will not be forgotten.

A prospectus will be issued in a few days, stating the changes and improvements contemplated for the ensuing year.

Boston, Dec. 15th, 1834. Sarah J. Hale

Sarah Hale was succeeding, however, while a number of other magazine attempts had failed. She had the goodwill of many New England newspapers, and some had given her magazine free publicity. For January 1, 1828, the New Hampshire *Spectator* carried this note:

Subscriptions for Mrs. Hale's *Ladies Magazine* will be received at this office. We cannot refrain from expressing a hope that those of our citizens who can afford it will come forward and subscribe for the work. It is the best way in which they can testify their respect for a lady, of whose talents and virtues we may all entertain a just pride.

The January 29, 1828, issue stated "we have received the first number of this work [the *Ladies' Magazine*] conducted by Mrs. Hale, author of *Northwood*. . . . It is published once a month and contains 48 octavo pages of very neat letterpress printing besides an advertising sheet. Price $3 per annum."

Thus New Hampshire friends were reminded of their former neighbor's latest effort.

At the same time Louis E. Godey had been advertising his

Lady's Book widely in New England. Godey was well aware of the *American Ladies' Magazine* and of its editor. Her *Traits of American Life* had been reviewed favorably in *The Lady's Book* in 1835. Five years before, this magazine had been started by Mr. Godey, a New York businessman, who believed the time had come for a modern magazine designed especially for women. He edited it himself for several years and denied no reasonable request of his readers (all "fair ladies" to Godey). He even acceded to some slightly *un*reasonable requests! One woman asked for "another description of Love than that found in the February number." "This shall be done," Godey promised, "and another fair Lady has it now in charge."

But the editorial side of the magazine was becoming too much for this farseeing publisher, whose bent was more toward the promotion and business end of publishing. And he set out to find a new editor for his *Book*. He had read Sarah Hale's *American Ladies' Magazine* and recognized her as an energetic, enterprising editor with good taste. He decided to ask her to edit his publication. By buying out her magazine in 1837, he at one stroke wiped out a competitor and acquired a skilled, crusading editor with nine years' experience.

"At large expense," he announced in July, 1836, he had engaged "ladies and gentlemen of the highest literary reputation in the country" to insure that the *"Lady's Book* will be principally composed of original matter of the best kind to be procured in this country and purely American in character." When his magazine merged with Sarah Hale's, he advertised it as "the oldest periodical of the kind in the United States." More, he promised the husbands of his readers that the *Book* would not undermine their position; they would find their wives "no less assiduous for his [the husband's] reception, or less sincere in welcoming his return" for having read the *Lady's Book*! Sarah Hale, adding her own comments, pointed out to men the benefits they and their children would receive as a result of better education for women, and she also pledged, in her new position, that nothing would be introduced "to undermine those sacred relations of domestic life, in which the Creator has placed the sceptre of woman's empire."

In a sense, Godey was walking a financial tightrope, for there were few advertisements in magazines of that day; all profits had to come from sales or subscriptions. And although to Godey the signs were clear that there was need for a magazine for women, its content had to be inoffensive to the male side of the family.

The word "magazine" originally meant "storehouse," and Godey had followed that meaning, offering a miscellany of what he thought would interest women—until Sarah J. Hale joined his staff. The new *Lady's Book* was to appeal to an audience that no previous magazine had attempted to reach—an audience of newly literate, middle- or upper-class women, who wanted to hear about new ideas and conveniences as well as fashion, who wanted to improve their minds. Sarah Hale's editing would insure that.

"New Era Commenced" was the headline when their joint editorship began. Subscribers were told that the quality of the paper and the printing would also be improved.

Two restrictions Godey insisted upon: Religion and politics were to be excluded and nothing that would in any way embarrass his "fair ladies" or shock their sensibilities must be permitted to taint the pages of the *Lady's Book*.

One problem presented itself to the new editor. Godey's publishing house was in Philadelphia. Her oldest son, David Emerson Hale, a West Point graduate, had been sent to Florida to serve in the war against the Seminole Indians. Her second son, Horatio, was about to graduate from Harvard College. Her daughters, Sarah and Frances Ann, were attending Emma Willard's Female Seminary in Troy, New

York. Soon all her children would be educated and ready to step into lives or careers of their own. But at the moment they were scattered, and she wished to maintain a home for her youngest son, William, until he had completed his courses at Harvard College. For this reason she delayed the move to Philadelphia, and Louis Godey graciously agreed that she might edit the magazine from Boston until that time. This was a generous concession in view of what must have been long and frustrating delays in the preparation and arrival of copy and articles for the magazine, which even in those leisurely times had deadlines to be met.

Shortly after his graduation in 1837, Horatio Hale, who had already written a scientific paper on the Indian languages, joined the first United States Exploring Expedition under Charles Wilkes of the U.S. Navy. The expedition was to conduct scientific observations as well as explore the South Seas and would be out of touch with civilization for at least four years. Horatio was the philologist of the expedition and its youngest member. Other young scientists going along were: James Dwight Dana, the naturalists Charles Pickering and Titian Peale (son of artist Charles Willson Peale), conchologist Joseph P. Couthouy, and horticulturalist William D. Brackenridge.

While Horatio was away on this daring and dangerous voyage, which eventually traced the coast of Antarctica and charted the Columbia River, Sarah Hale received the news of her oldest son's death. The army had transferred David from service in the South to the Canadian border. The sudden change of climate brought on hemorrhages and he died at Plattsburg, New York, in the spring of 1839, at the age of twenty-five.

This blow prostrated Sarah and left her in no frame of mind to undergo the anxiety and fatigue of moving to a new and unfamiliar city. She wanted to stay close to her youngest son, William, at all costs and explained this to Louis Godey, asking him to be patient: "It is not a common loss that I mourn. I depended on him [David] as a friend. . . . I cannot, at once, summon fortitude to enter on the occupations of a world so dark and desolate as this now appears."

Godey was an understanding man (like Dickens's Mr. Pickwick in appearance and character), and he agreed. Sarah would remain in Boston until William had finished his work at Harvard in 1841.

Despite her grief over David's death and her concern about Horatio's dangerous mission, Sarah was very much in control of her feelings. Her restraint is evident in a letter to her friend Eliza Leslie in April 1841. She remarks that for four months she had not had any letter from Horatio, but "the last news from the exploring expedition represents all in good health. I feel very anxious to learn that the vessels have safely returned from their southern exploration."

When she moved to Philadelphia that summer, she knew that it would be a long time yet before Horatio returned. Then an officer wrote her the following message on October 30, 1841:

> U.S. Ship Vincennes,
> Bay of San Francisco
>
> Madam:
> Believing it will afford you pleasure to hear from your son H. Hale Esq. through me, as he may not have been aware of the present opportunity to forward letters to you, I take the liberty of informing you that he remains in Oregon Territory for a few weeks . . . then proceeds to this Port. After spending two or three months in this interesting country he will proceed to Mexico. . . . Captain Wilkes gave him these orders in compliance with his request, as he was of the opinion that he would be able to gain much valuable information. . . .

Little was known then about California (there was as yet no city or town of San Francisco), Oregon Territory or Mexico—the places for which Horatio was bound. They were said to be the haunt of the wild "mountainy men," guides, and traders in beaver and hides (for the hat and shoe factories of New England). Another young Harvard man, Richard Henry Dana, had just published *Two Years Before the Mast*, an account of his voyage around Cape Horn to California, and Sarah Hale must have read it. She also must have sought information in gazetteers and on maps. But it required much faith to wait serenely for her son's return. Meanwhile, the magazine demanded her attention.

7

Publishing in Philadelphia

What did Philadelphia offer to the new editor of Godey's *Lady's Book*?

The city was the magazine capital of the United States, after ten years of prestige as the national capital. In Philadelphia stood the Carpenter's Hall, where George Washington, John Adams, and many other ardent Americans had met and argued through the Continental and Constitutional Congresses.

With a population of some 220,000, Philadelphia was considered "the Athens of America," by some. Others strongly disputed this, particularly those who came from Boston or New York, a city that was fast becoming a strong rival in the journalistic field.

Philadelphia offered one of the finest libraries in the United States, as well as one of the country's oldest institutions "to promote useful knowledge," the American Philosophical Society, founded by Benjamin Franklin. In Philadelphia, too, one might view the assembled bones of the first mastodon found in America, in the first science museum. This museum and an academy for artists had been established by painter Charles Willson Peale, whose son Titian, like Sarah's Horatio, was with the Wilkes expedition.

On Chestnut Street Sarah and her daughters might stroll

by Philadelphia's fashionable shops, stop to rest, and sip an ice at Roussel's, one of the first soda fountains in the country.

Philadelphia was warmer than Boston, and more humid. The streets were as narrow or even narrower, except for a few wide avenues such as Market Street. Sarah wrote a bit later of this city of brick that its heat in summer was enough to "test . . . the powers of a salamander."

She found a house with room enough for herself, two daughters, and two sons, when they were all at home. Like many of Boston's Beacon Hill houses, the brick town houses here were built close to the sidewalk, with wrought-iron railings and narrow white marble steps.

Philadelphia had become the home of many writers, artists, engravers, and others who worked for the magazines. John Greenleaf Whittier, a New Englander, whose poem, "Spirit of the North," Sarah had published when he was twenty-two and still in college, was working here on the *Pennsylvania Freeman*. Thomas Sully, a leading portrait painter, was here, and Darley, whose wood engravings illustrated many children's books. Another resident was John Sartain, an Englishman, who was earning a reputation as one of America's foremost engravers.

Sarah's employer, Louis Godey, lived at 534 North Sixth Street with his wife and his five children and entertained many distinguished people there. Edgar Allan Poe said, "No man has warmer friends or fewer enemies."

In addition to Sarah Hale, Godey had engaged the name, if not the exclusive output of one of the most popular women writers of the day, Lydia H. Sigourney. Like her co-editor, Lydia Sigourney was of New England birth (Norwich, Connecticut) and wrote for many of the popular magazines and gift annuals. She had produced several best sellers, including *How to Be Happy* and *Letters to Young Ladies* (1833) and was quite as well-known as Sarah Hale as a producer of a ceaseless fountain of verse. The writer Henry

James, in a later period, described her rather unkindly as "glossily ringletted and monumentally breast-pinned." She and Sarah Hale were already on friendly terms.

Matthew Carey, a leading book publisher, had his offices in Philadelphia, and Sarah had business dealings with him and with his partners. The poet and painter Thomas Buchanan Read came to Philadelphia in 1846 and began contributing to Godey's *Lady's Book*. Sarah became well acquainted with these personalities and others. She knew and corresponded with most of the literary "names" of that era.

Sarah looked forward with some curiosity to her first meeting with the young poet Edgar Allan Poe, who was then living in Philadelphia. She remembered his early work, *Al Aaraaf*, which she had appraised correctly. More than that, Poe was a link with her beloved son David; the two young men had been classmates at West Point. It was through David that she had seen Poe's early poems, and however fleeting their friendship Sarah would not forget it. She might first have seen Poe lingering to read his letters under the shade trees of Independence Square or met him by chance in Mr. Peale's exhibition rooms.

This was one of the rare hopeful periods in Poe's life. He found rents in Phildelphia reasonable and food plentiful, and his delicate wife, Virginia, seemed to be in better health. He was working on Graham's Magazine as assistant editor (at a salary of $800 a year) and was even planning and looking forward to a magazine of his own to be called *The Penn*. As an editor on *Graham's* he was in competition with Sara. There was keen rivalry for the work of good writers, and Poe was a discriminating editor. However hard-pressed himself for time and money, he seldom compromised on quality. In this he had the support of his publisher, Graham, who, like Godey, sought "to build up a native literature by purchasing at adequate prices the work of the best American writers," unlike those "piratical publishers who, at practically no cost to themselves, made periodicals by running their dragnets through the pages of European books and magazines."

Sarah, in her elegant black silk gown, and the poet, always neatly dressed, a dark mantle draped over his shoulders, must have attracted many eyes as they walked on Chestnut Street or greeted one another in front of the magazine office. They agreed about the serious threats to authors' work through lack of a copyright law; they often discussed commissions for more articles by Poe, debated who the best printers and engravers were, and talked about the state of Virginia's health. Sarah listened to Poe with respect and with sympathy for his problems, and held out to him the same encouragement she had given to others who had come to her for advice. People striving to rise above adversity quickly won her heart and help. Perhaps, in her office, Poe read aloud to her "some poem or weird tale in a voice that seemed to summon presences from the shadows" (to quote his biographer, Hervey Allen).

Since Poe was obviously fascinated by the hot and icy lands then being explored in the South Seas, Horatio Hale's voyage would have interested him greatly. A few years before he had published the *Narrative of Arthur Gordon Pym*, based on firsthand reports of an earlier voyage to the same regions. It was a haunting story, culminating in the treachery of natives of unknown Antarctic islands; and it may well have given Sarah Hale some uneasiness, for news of the wreck of one of the smaller ships in Wilkes's expedition had come back, though she had no way of knowing whether her son had been aboard. It was certainly a time that called for all her faith. The Wilkes expedition had started off poorly equipped, as it turned out, and the ship *Peacock*, already damaged by ice, was wrecked while trying to enter the Columbia River on July 18, 1841. Luckily no lives were lost. Sarah's poem of thanksgiving, "The Wreck of the Peacock," commemorates the incident.

Poe and Sarah Hale and Godey also met at the lavish

literary parties held at the home of the publisher Graham. Graham's dining room was remembered by many of those who gathered there for its scintillating crystal chandelier, filled with candles that were reflected in a room full of mirrors. There wine flowed in abundance, and the conversation lasted until the candles burnt low toward midnight.

8

Women Invade Literature

Although Sarah Hale enjoyed dining out and going to the theater, there were always stacks of manuscripts still to be read; and she did read them, not merely a few pages but through to the end, before deciding whether or not to publish them. There was plenty of other editorial drudgery, too—reading and correcting proofs, checking the use of words, about which she was most particular, and other exacting details.

With three editors, Godey would seem to have had a large enough staff—perhaps too large. The names of Sarah Hale, Lydia Sigourney, and Eliza Leslie all appear as editors on the title pages of 1841 issues. Because of her popular appeal, Godey retained Lydia Sigourney for several years as a co-editor, paying her $500 a year, whether she contributed anything to the magazine or not. However, after 1842 the Sigourney name was dropped.

Lydia Sigourney symbolized the purity of true womanhood that Godey sought to maintain as the standard for his magazine. "Nothing having the slightest appearance of indelicacy," he told one would-be contributor, "shall ever be admitted to the *Lady's Book*." Lydia Sigourney wrote, for example, a book entitled *Whisper to a Bride*, bound in white moire and intended to be given to young women when they married. But, a later commentator reports, "as far as intimate information was concerned, there was no need to whisper, since the book contained none at all."

As mother and wife, woman must strive, Lydia Sigourney sighed, "to bear the evils and sorrows which may be appointed us, with a patient mind. . . . It seems, indeed, to be expected of us; since the passive and enduring virtues are more immediately within our province." (*Letters to Mothers*, Hartford, 1838) Nevertheless, much to the chagrin of her grudging husband, Mrs. Sigourney turned out to be the breadwinner in her own family.

Eliza Leslie was an assistant editor. She won her way into print first with a successful cookbook; then Godey's *Book* published her prize-winning story, "Mrs. Washington Potts," in 1832. Many readers enjoyed the quiet humor in her writing, and this same story was reprinted as late as 1866. The sister of Charles Robert Leslie, a well-known artist, she was also the author of several best sellers on cookery and etiquette. She established her own *Miss Leslie's Magazine* for children in 1843, although continuing to contribute to Godey's.

About this time Morton McMichael was added to the staff as a general assistant to Mr. Godey.

Alice B. Neal was a contributor and sometimes assistant editor. She was the wife of the author of "Charcoal Sketches," Joseph C. Neal, who persuaded Miriam Berry Whitcher to write for Godey's *Book* what were considered the best Yankee dialect stories that had yet been written.

> If all the trees in all the woods were men,
> And each and every blade of grass a pen;
>
> . . .
>
> And for ten thousand ages, day and night,
> The human race should write, and write, and write,

Till all the pens and paper were used up,
And the huge inkstand was an empty cup,
Still would the scribblers clustered round its brink
Call for more pens, more paper, and more ink.

So wrote Oliver Wendell Holmes in "Cacoëthes Scribendi." And if the last word in the first line were changed to *women*, it would be an accurate picture of his times. It was overwhelmingly, unquestionably the heyday of the female poet and novelist.

The mainstay of many of the magazines was what Hawthorne disdainfully called the "mob of scribbling women," who specialized in high-flown sentiment, high morals, and poetical effusions. The galling thing to Hawthorne and other male writers was that these women produced poetry and prose that sold in scores of thousands while his stories seldom sold ten thousand copies. Hawthorne did not realize that markets (and larger book sales) were to be found in the raw new towns and cities to the West and were determined by access to navigable waterways and more rapid modes of transportation. This is why New York and Philadelphia developed so rapidly as publishing centers at this time. Transportation was important—as well as appealing subject matter.

Travelers from abroad noticed, by the mid-eighteenth century, the growing influence of women in American life, even in the West. As soon as wives and women teachers arrived on the scene, bringing with them books and copies of Godey's *Book*, standards of discipline and morality were raised.

In the 1830s, and 1840s, women in America were restless, no longer content with timeworn roles. They were seeking to express themselves; they began literary careers with poetry, essays, and fiction in local newspapers; then expanded into magazines and books. They defied the convention that said women could not speak in public. They did speak out against slavery, against inhumane conditions in prisons and hospitals; against intemperance; against their own "nonexistence"; and for more education.

Lucy Larcom, who worked for a time in a spinning factory in Lowell, Massachusetts, and wrote poetry in spare moments, later went West to teach in the new schools opening there. She said of her New England girlhood: "We were taught to work almost as if it were a religion, to keep at work, expecting nothing else. . . . The children of old New England were always surrounded, it is true, with stubborn matter of fact—the hand to hand struggle for existence. But that was no hindrance. Poetry must have prose to root itself in; the homelier its earth-spot, the lovelier, by contrast its heaven-breathing flowers." This was also reflected in Sarah Josepha Hale's life. It was the poems she sent to New England newspapers that led to her literary career.

Women's entrance into "serious" endeavors may have been discouraged, but when it came to writing, they were irresistible. As early as 1828 the New York *Mirror* commented on women's *editorial* ability:

> Much as our gallantry induced us to praise the novel attempts of ladies assuming the responsibility of editors . . . we were not prepared for such a display of talent and judgment as they have exhibited. There is, indeed, a splendid galaxy of female literati—or shall we say literata—in our country. The productions of Mesdames Calvin, Dumont, Hale, Muzzy, Sedgwick, Sigourney, Thayre, Ware, and others will add interest to any page they adorn. Boston is the favourite seat of the lady-muses.

Not only were women doing the editing and writing but, reported *Graham's Magazine* in 1844, the so-called "light magazines" were "training a host of young writers and creating an army of readers." And they were *women* readers eager to be led, entertained, and educated.

After years of pent-up talents, women at last seemed to be bursting their bonds. Their creative powers *would* be expressed! Not only was there a psychological need for self-realization, long felt, but there was an economic need, too. The horizon for women's work had to be expanded. Women found that men did not always prove to be the strong "protectors" they had been led to believe in. Men's business judgment could be lacking, their trust in a partner misplaced; men could be deceived and deceitful, cruel and tyrannical. So if a woman had any talent and wished to keep her home and clothe her children, she ought to cultivate her talents, practice them, and keep them well-honed.

In July 1830, in Sarah Hale's *American Ladies' Magazine*, a report was made of a survey taken in New York, Baltimore, and Philadelphia on the subject of "Female Wages," mainly among seamstresses. Not surprisingly, it was found that "their earnings were not sufficient for their support." Again Sarah Hale was calling attention to the neglected status of working women.

Thousands of farm-bred girls applied to the new factories for employment, and well-educated but shyer types, like Susan Warner, Frances Hodgson, and Louisa Alcott also sought an acceptable way of making an income. The Hodgson family were emigrants from England, living in "reduced circumstances" in Tennessee, when occasional copies of Godey's *Lady's Book* and Peterson's *Magazine* were loaned them "by more fortunate Knoxville friends who could afford such luxuries." Frances read them avidly, with special attention to the editor's replies to would-be contributors.

"Poring over these curt remarks, there grew in Frances' imagination the fixed impression that an editor was a species of autocrat who made arbitrary rules about the submission of manuscripts." Nevertheless, the pinch of poverty and some innate desire for expression enabled the shy seventeen-year-old girl to conquer her misgivings. Did the magazines *pay* for those stories of unrequited love, self-sacrifice, and high life in Philadelphia or London or Newport? Could Frances afford even the postage to send in one of her stories? She recalled the bleak words from the editor's column: "We cannot receive MSS. on which insufficient postage has been paid." At last her family's continuing poverty drove her into action. After the most painstaking preparations she copied one of her stories in longhand and wrote an accompanying letter to the editor, "a wonder of concise brevity":

> Sir: I enclose stamps for the return of the accompanying MSS., "Miss Desborough's Difficulties," if you do not find it suitable for publication in your magazine. My object is remuneration.
>
> Yours respectfully,
> F. Hodgson.

Note that last, tight-lipped word—"remuneration." Thus was the career of Frances Hodgson (later Burnett) launched.

Her first story, "Hearts and Diamonds," appeared in Godey's *Book* for June 1868, and a second story had been accepted. Frances Hodgson was a published authoress at the age of eighteen. It is hard to say which was more exciting, seeing her work in print or being able to buy alpaca for new dresses for her sister and herself, the first in a long time.

Sarah Josepha Hale, engraved after a portrait by W.B. Chambers, published in Godey's *Lady's Book*, December 1850. By permission of the Harvard College Library

An early view of Sarah Josepha Hale's birthplace, Newport, New Hampshire. From a drawing by Henry E. Baldwin

Quincy Hall Market, where the fair for the benefit of Bunker Hill Monument was held. It was built in 1825 under the improvement program of Mayor Josiah Quincy. Courtesy State Street Bank & Trust Company

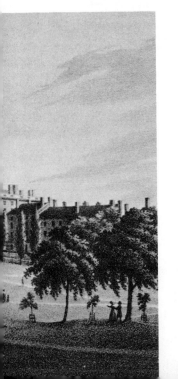

Boston Common as it looked in 1830, dominated by the state house designed by Charles Bulfinch. On the left of the state house is John Hancock's mansion, which was demolished several decades later. The large square mansion with many chimneys on the right was built by Thomas Amory. Much of this building still stands, now occupied by stores and offices. Courtesy State Street Bank & Trust Company

GODEY'S

LADY'S BOOK.

PHILADELPHIA, JANUARY, 1857.

RAMBLES ABOUT THE CITY.

BY FLORENCE FASHIONHUNTER.

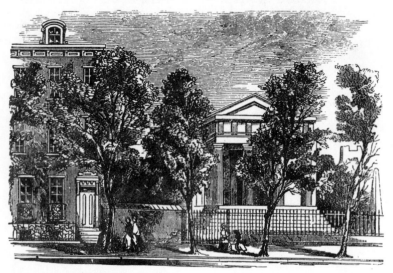

CHURCH OF THE EPIPHANY. AND RESIDENCE OF MR. GODEY.

> "When I walk out on Chestnut Street.
> Bobbing around, around, around
> Something new I always meet.
> As I go bobbing around '

COME, reader, we will take a walk. Not that bonnet, if you please, my dear madam; that is a very pretty little affair—for some other occasion; but now you must don your most *recherché chapeau*, assume a thrilling mantle, "sport" your moire antique dress, draw on immaculate gaiter-boots and kid-gloves, raise a most fashionable parasol, and now, if you are as charmingly arrayed as your wardrobe will permit, we will start. Allons! Presto! Pass'

You see, without the aid of railroad or telegraph, we are on the Broadway of Philadelphia, Chestnut Street; where fashion, folly, pleasure, and business reign in turn, and the beaux and belles display the latest fashions, smallest bonnets, and largest moustaches, and "kill time" by promenading from Fourth to Tenth Street, to the tune of

> "Here we go up, up, upy,
> And here we go down, down, downy !"

Great subject for a moral lecture this fashionable waste of time, but you and I have not time to moralize, for here we are in front of the Baptist Church above Nineteenth Street.

11

Full page from Godey's *Lady's Book* showing the Godey residence on Chestnut Street, Philadelphia, next to the Church of the Epiphany.

Thomas C. Corner's portrait of Edgar Allan Poe as he looked when Sarah J. Hale knew him. Courtesy Enoch Pratt Free Library, Baltimore, Maryland

Louis A. Godey, from an engraving published in the *Lady's Book*, February 1850. By permission of the Harvard College Library

In 1865 calisthenics classes at Mount Holyoke featured exercises with rings, weights, and Indian clubs. Courtesy Williston Memorial Library, Mount Holyoke College

Mount Holyoke Female Seminary as it looked when Emily Dickinson attended. Courtesy Williston Memorial Library, Mount Holyoke College

Sketch of Elizabeth Blackwell, M.D., by the Contessa Charnacee, 1859.
Courtesy Hobart & William Smith Colleges

Fashion plate for Godey's *Lady's Book* of 1875 showing the latest typewriter by Travis of Philadelphia.

According to nineteenth-century fashion arbiters "This garment, combining the chemise and drawers, has very many advantages. We recommend it especially to ladies traveling, to those giving out their wash, and to ladies boarding. It is also decidedly cooler for summer."

9

A New Era

A marked improvement in the contents of the *Lady's Book* was noticeable as soon as Sarah Hale took up the editorial reins in Philadelphia. Louis Godey, and those who worked for him, sometimes had found it hard to refuse the wheedling writers who poured out their hearts in fountains of watery verse and sugary romances. It was, after all, the age of the weeping willow and the embroidered penwiper. But Sarah looked at their offerings with a more experienced, if not jaundiced, eye. She did not hesitate to list the titles of unacceptable articles or stories in the Editor's Table, preceded by the statement, "We have no room for the following," thus letting their authors know that they should try elsewhere.

She occasionally entered a plea for patience because "a large roll of manuscript remains unread." She cautioned, too: "The character of the *Lady's Book* requires that a high standard of moral and literary excellence be sustained." Here are some of her comments on manuscripts submitted:

"Too flowery."

"The subject is worn out."

"The writing is cramped and writing *in blue ink on blue paper* is a trial of patience which we hope Job never had to endure."

Among the popular authors whose works appeared more or less regularly were Poe, the ever-present Lydia Sigourney, T. S. Arthur, Grace Greenwood, Thomas Buchanan Read, and William Gilmore Simms, whose stories of American frontier life were compared favorably to James Fenimore Cooper's. Simms's short stories and novels are appreciated more today as a worthy contribution to American literature.

Nathaniel Parker Willis, a popular writer of light fiction, travel articles, and "hurrygraphs," as he called them, divided his talents among the New York *Mirror*, *Graham's Magazine*, *Godey's* and the *Ladies' Companion*. He received $50 from *Godey's* for an article of four printed pages—a very high rate at that time. "*Graham's* and *Godey's* liberal prices," said Willis, "were like a sunrise" on the magazinists' world. His contributions to Godey's *Lady's Book* continued until 1850. Sarah Hale knew Willis in Boston, where he, too, had engaged in magazine work and edited an annual called *The Token*, to which she also contributed. His sister, whose work he scathingly rejected, became the best-selling author Fanny Fern, having set out to defy his judgment! Some of her work is still in print. His father had established the famous *Youth's Companion* magazine, but young Willis wanted to make his own mark, and did, from New York, not Boston. "The mines of Golconda would not tempt me to return and live in Boston," he wrote. Poe, Hawthorne, and other writers were also looking to New York now for greater appreciation and sale of their work.

Grace Greenwood sent in travel pieces and articles and became an editorial assistant in 1849, but her contributions to Godey's *Book* were discontinued when her antislavery sentiments became known. It would not do to alienate southern subscribers.

Apart from its choice of editors and writers and its policy of avoiding controversial issues, there were several reasons why Godey's *Book* was successful: First, Godey published the names of his contributors and paid the well-known writers adequate fees—usually much better than those paid by competing periodicals. Previously unpublished writers often had to be content with the prestige of appearing in print—in Godey's *Lady's Book*—a practice not unknown even today.

Second, Godey copyrighted the magazine from 1845 on, thus insuring his writers (and himself) as much as possible against piracy. Publishers of weeklies or other periodicals, accustomed to purloining stories from *Godey's* and other monthly magazines, became enraged as they saw their best sources of material cut off!

Third, Godey published his magazine *promptly*, at a time when everything had to be done by hand, a remarkable achievement. Even today, with high-speed presses, magazines do not always come out on time. Delivery to the subscriber, via the U.S. mails, was another problem, for which the publisher could not be held responsible.

Fourth, Godey sought out the best engravers and illustrators and featured colored fashion plates. He even sent artists abroad to copy the latest fashions in France and England. Since there was no color printing then, women were employed to hand-color the plates at the rate of two cents each. This also enabled Godey to maintain that his entire magazine was prepared by women (except the printing—but even here women compositors were being hired in some shops). Beginning with one fashion plate every three months, the publisher added to their quantity as their popularity—and his income—grew until, in 1849, he printed as many as twenty colored plates.

In addition, "embellishments" or steel and copper engravings were added to complement the text. C. R. Leslie, E. G. Leutze, S. F. B. Morse, W. S. Mount, Thomas Sully, and R. W. Weir were some of the artists used. These embellishments, as well as music, dress patterns, and woodcuts, were bound together, usually at the front of the magazine. Subscribers frequently removed them and had the pictures framed for home decoration, and there is still a demand for old Godey's *Book* fashion plates.

This was the golden age of the fashion plate. It seemed as if the delicate heroines and languishing heroes of the sentimental stories were portrayed in the unreal world of the fashion plates that appeared with them in Godey's *Book*. Ladies' dresses for every occasion, time of day, and year, were shown and, in later issues, with appropriate backgrounds. The plates bore such captions as "The New Baby Admired by His Twelve-Year-Old Sister," and "Will He Never Come?" a scene showing two young women with flowers in their ringlets wearing ball gowns and gently yearning expressions.

In 1838 Godey's ran a colored sketch of Queen Victoria before her coronation, simply dressed in a full-skirted black, taffetalike gown with train. On her hair rested a gold-pointed tiara. Sarah Hale's accompanying article dealt less with fashion than with Victoria's moral influence: "To us American women the most interesting act she has performed is the unobtrusive one recognizing female talent. She has, we understand, pensioned from her private purse three eminent literary ladies, Miss Joanna Baillie, Miss Edgeworth and Miss Mitford." This augured well for the cause of women writers in Victoria's reign.

Although herself like a fashion plate (her grandchildren remembered her regal bearing), Sarah Hale was not the fashion editor. Opposed to extravagance in fashion, she did not like to see Americans apeing the tastes of Europe and deplored the effect on health of the tightly laced corsets women endured to produce the fashionable wasp waist.

Sarah stated her opinions on "The Mode" in *Traits of American Life*. She resisted women's usual reliance on the ever-changing fashions of Paris and London and advocated a national American costume "which would, wherever an American appeared, announce him as a republican, and the countryman of Washington. The men would probably do this if ladies would lead the way."

In any case, "we would not have ladies despise or neglect dress. They should be *always* fit to be seen; personal neatness is indispensable to agreeableness—almost to virtue. A proper portion of time and attention must scrupulously be given to external appearance, but not the whole of our days and energies."

Her earliest statement of policy on fashions in the *Ladies' Magazine* was: "Our engraving of the 'Fashions' . . . is not given as a pattern for imitation, but as a study for each reader to examine and decide how far this costume is appropriate to her own figure, face and circumstances. This exercise of individual taste is sadly neglected by our fair countrywomen." Sarah Hale held to the good rule that fashion must be adapted to the wearer. While today's couturiers and fashion leaders have confirmed her good judgment, she was going against the tide of her time. Harriet Beecher Stowe recognized this when she wrote, "The idea of presenting at one and the same time fashions and a healthful, well proportioned female figure, is a new and original one, of which your magazine may be justly proud. I hope you will have the grace and strength to go through with it."

Another exclusive feature of Godey's *Book* was its translations of French fashion terms. It was Sarah Hale who introduced the word *lingerie* to American women. The word became an accepted designation for women's intimate apparel, night gowns, and robes. "We adopt the term," she wrote in September 1852, "as many other French phrases have been incorporated into the vocabulary of fashion, because it best expresses what we wish to describe; for under this head comes every garment that we here denominate 'plain sewing' . . . or 'white work' . . . everything of the under wardrobe."

Fundamental, of course, to a presentable, attractive appearance is a healthy body, and Sarah frequently reminded readers of this. In her book, *Manners*, she advocated outdoor sports for women, such as horseback riding, skating, croquet, and archery. Even dancing might be the source of "beautiful effects which may spring from the right use of this innocent recreation," she felt. This, too, was a rather bold viewpoint, since many religions and sections of the public frowned upon dancing.

Among Godey's *Book's* features was a music department. Since Sarah Hale approved of dancing as both exercise and a graceful accomplishment, instructions for the polka, "this elegant and fashionable dance," and the waltz were included in 1845 issues of the magazine. The waltz had scandalized some sections of society until Victoria herself danced to the music played for her by Johann Strauss during a great court ball at Buckingham Palace, just before her coronation as queen of England. In fact, Strauss wrote the Victoria Waltz for her.

Godey's *Book* also marked the popularity of the Swedish singer Jenny Lind by publishing her song, "Hear Me, Maiden, Hear Me, While I Sue!"

Most of the new women's seminaries included some form of calisthenics or physical education for their students. Emma Willard's school, which Sarah Hale's daughters attended, offered exercise and dancing daily and introduced a course in physiology.

Frances Wright, the English reformer who visited America about this time, held that women should pay more attention to their health, should exercise as men do; "to invigorate the body is to invigorate the mind." Some magazines, including Godey's, printed illustrations of women doing calisthenics.

And in Godey's for July 1841, the costume a doctor advocated for young girls while exercising was not very different from that made famous later by Mrs. Amelia Bloomer. The designer of the "bloomer" costume, Elizabeth Smith Miller, said she "adopted the short skirt, after years of annoyance. . . . Working in my garden . . . in bedraggled skirts that clung in fettering folds about my feet and ankles, I became desperate and resolved on immediate release. With the short skirt I wore Turkish trousers, but these soon gave place to the straight pantaloon which was much better adapted to walking through the snow-drifted roads of my country home." This was in the 1850s.

The *Lady's Book* was Godey's favorite project, and he clearly was inordinately proud of it. Every column he wrote for the magazine beams and glows with pride of ownership, as can be seen in the following, written in 1839:

> You will find in no English magazine such a store of entertainment. We were the first to introduce the system of calling forth the slumbering talent of our country by offering an equivalent for the efforts of genius. Our subscription list now doubles the list of any other magazine in America. A few years ago the *Lady's Book* had not an original article in its columns, with but eight steel plates per annum and four plates of fashion on copper; now it is entirely original and includes the first names of the day, and its embellishments surpass any other magazine of double the price. Nor must our readers suppose we have exhausted our stock of contributions from our lady writers.

Louis Godey was constantly having to fight against the flattery of being imitated. If he published four fashion plates per issue, *Graham's* would publish eight. If he introduced a folded insert, *Graham's* (or some other periodical) would soon follow suit with an inferior copy, always inferior because Godey's *Book* was first, first in initiative, quality, and popularity with its women readers. Godey's standards of excellence were always being moved a notch or two higher, ever challenging to his editorial staff, and chiefly to Sarah J. Hale, who was responsible for the bulk of the literary content. Even the severest critic of the magazines of the day, Edgar Allan Poe, had a good word to say for Godey's *Book* in a survey of "Our Magazine Literature" published in *The New World* for March 4, 1843. He called it "a clever magazine for the entertainment of ladies" and felt it would be unique if "the productions of gentlemen were excluded altogether. Some of the stories published are exceedingly good, but the majority of them are 'stale, flat and unprofitable.' A certain portion of sentimental nonsense is quite indispensable, but it would be well to make this portion as small as possible. . . . Let fewer stories be written and more essays—a less quantity of rhyme and more true poetry."

In a full-page advertisement for the magazine that appeared in Godey's *Book* for 1850, Sarah J. Hale's name was prominently featured. Under Our Reading Matter, Godey stated:

> We have long stood at the head of the magazine world for our contributions; they are always moral and instructive, and such as may be placed before a family without hesitation. This department is under the control of Mrs. Sarah Josepha Hale, whose name alone is a sufficient guarantee for the propriety of the *Lady's Book*. We may say the same of our engravings. We will never, as is done by a contemporary, publish indecent model-artist pic-

tures, such as no parent would allow a child to look
at.
GODEY'S LADY'S BOOK for 1850 SHALL
SURPASS THAT of 1849, and exceed all magazines
past, present, and to come.

10

Education for Life,
Not "Nonexistence"

Sarah Hale rejoiced in 1844 that "the *Book* is taken, as their heart's friend, by the young and lovely." The *Book* had indeed been taken to the hearts and had fed the aspirations of many women, including those teen-age girls who worked in the spinning rooms and shoe factories of Lowell and Lynn, Massachusetts. The mill girls were great readers, keeping a book in their pockets or on a nearby windowsill to study or ponder when they were not needed at their machines. They published a magazine of their own, too, *The Lowell Offering.*

Many of these girls worked twelve or fourteen hours a day either to earn further schooling for themselves or for the college education of their brothers. Lucy Larcom, the Cape Ann poet, remembered reading tales by Harriet E. Beecher (Stowe) and poems by Holmes, Poe, and Longfellow in Godey's and Graham's magazines.

So Sarah's exhortations for better education for women struck a response in young girls in all walks of life. And some of these same mill girls took up teaching when the call came for teachers to go West and help civilize the wilderness.

From the very beginning of her editorship Sarah Hale had felt that the education of girls and women was of first importance. As early as December 1832, her *Ladies' Magazine* gave information about infant schools and schools for young women, then known as "female seminaries." She offered guidance to parents about to go to this expense, remarking that "our Female Seminaries are very expensive—it costs more now to educate a daughter *fashionably* than a son *liberally*." She published selections from Emma Willard's lectures, including one important lesson on the transience of wealth and political power, urging women to provide themselves "with resources against a day of change."

It was not fashion that she advocated but the kind of education provided in, for example, Miss Fiske's School for Young Ladies, in Keene, New Hampshire. This school taught nearly all branches of learning, as well as drawing, painting, and plain and ornamental needlework.

On the school's twentieth anniversary Sarah Hale again cited its excellence in her magazine, noting the increased prosperity it had brought to the town of Keene and the "refined taste and literary tone it has diffused over the society of that charming village," which was "beyond the value of dollars and cents." Yet Catherine Fiske had maintained high standards in her school with little profit to herself, and, in her now-advancing age, Sarah felt that she deserved some outside support.

Miss Fiske maintained that "woman is not personally placed at the head of our national government—but the state of the moral atmosphere of our country depends on her influence, which is deeply felt in every domestic realm; where, if woman legislates with care, justice, kindness, and wisdom, the subjects will generally be virtuous and happy;—but females may be so educated as not to be qualified to rule or obey; they may be feeble, inefficient, and unhappy—rendered so by an undue attachment to frivolous books, and elegant trifles—a love of incessant change, and feverish excitement, etc., and by yielding to the influence of vanity, and the tyranny of fashion." Miss Fiske always educated for usefulness, rather than show.

Godey's *Lady's Book* kept its readers up to date on the location, quality, and progress of the female seminaries, wherever they existed. Among those that later became colleges was Mount Holyoke at South Hadley, Massachusetts, founded by Mary Lyon in 1837. Emily Dickinson, unknown then, conquered her shyness enough to attend it for a year. "I have a very dear home," she wrote to a friend, "and this is my first trial in the way of absence for any length of time in my life." Yet she was happy, after the first bout of homesickness:

> The school is very large, and though quite a number have left, on account of finding the examinations more difficult than they anticipated, yet there are nearly 300 now. Perhaps you know that Miss Lyon is raising her standard of scholarship a good deal, on account of the number of applicants this year and . . . she makes the examinations more severe than usual. . . . I room with my cousin Emily, who is a senior. . . . Things seem much more like home than I anticipated and the teachers are all very kind and affectionate to us. . . . I will tell you my order of time for the day, as you were so kind as to give me yours. At 6 o'clock, we all rise. We breakfast at 7. Our study hours begin at 8. At 9 we all meet in Seminary Hall for devotions. At 10½ I recite a review of Ancient History in connection with which we read Goldsmith and Grimshaw. At 11 I recite a lesson in "Pope's Essay on Man" which is merely transposition. At 12 I practise Calisthenics and at 12¼ read until dinner which is at 12½. After dinner from 1½ until 2 I sing in Seminary Hall. From 2¾ until 3¾ I practise upon the Piano. At 3¾ I go to Section, where we give in all our accounts for the day, including Absence—Tardiness—Communi-

cations—Breaking Silent Study hours—Receiving Company in our rooms and ten thousand other things. . . . At 4½ we go into Seminary Hall and receive advice from Miss Lyon in the form of a lecture. We have supper at 6 and silent study hours from then until the retiring bell, which rings at 8¼ but the tardy bell does not ring until 9¾, so that we don't often obey the first warning to retire. One thing is certain and that is, that Miss Lyon and all the teachers seem to consult our comfort and happiness in everything they do and you know that is pleasant.

Sarah Hale's two daughters, enrolled at the Troy Female Academy conducted by Emma Willard, followed a similar schedule, but more time was devoted to study of the Bible and parents were requested to furnish their daughters with simply, plainly made dresses—no furbelows, laces, or jewelry.

To some girls examination time at the school would have been daunting, for the exams were public, attended not only by parents and friends but by prominent educators and others who cared to witness. Each class was examined thoroughly and for the most part orally. Some of the girls' best compositions were read aloud, though not by the authors themselves. It was a gala occasion for those who excelled, but harrowing for the less gifted and those who were shy. There were no final marks or honors; each girl knew in her heart and head whether she had done well or not.

Boston, Massachusetts, had a high school for girls in 1825, and more candidates for it than space could accommodate. But this school lasted only eighteen or nineteen months "during which not one pupil voluntarily quitted it, nor would as long as they could be allowed to stay, except in case of marriage." Mayor Quincy vetoed the funds for its continuance on the grounds that it was becoming too popular and too expensive to the city! The cost of each pupil was eleven dollars per year. This high school for girls was abolished despite public protest. In her *Ladies' Magazine* Sarah Hale had urged its reopening on an enlarged and permanent basis and advocated the regular training of women as teacher candidates.

Some twelve years later, in 1839, the state of Massachusetts matched funds with a generous individual to found the first normal school for women teachers in the United States. Sarah Hale's advocacy had helped to bring this about and she joyously announced that "the first Normal School was opened at Lexington a few weeks since for *Female Teachers!* . . . There is soon to be another . . . for males—but the precedence has, for once, been given in the walks of science to woman!"

Sarah published advice to mothers on children's reading and was always alert for suitable stories for children. She even compiled some of Mrs. A. L. Barbauld's stories for children, since there was a demand for them at that time. Sarah's own poems for children were among her most successful and were widely read in McGuffey's *Readers*, though often the poet's name was omitted.

How to Begin was the title of a column for parents that she wrote for the *Lady's Book*, and the advice is still good. Much of it was devoted to sensible attention to health, exercise and diet, clothing, and quotes from "a physician of Scotland." She later recommended a book by the French author L. Aimée-Martin on the education of mothers, suggesting that it be read five times, if possible in the original. Sarah Hale was impartial and global in her search for helpful advice on this topic.

Women had been excluded from too many activities, she

realized. Only because of the intensity of their interest in antislavery did they dare to attend public meetings or lectures. In Boston the Lowell Institute lectures were freely open to women, due to the influence of the founder's wife. And women made up a large part of the audience when Richard H. Dana and Ralph Waldo Emerson lectured.

When women without male escorts were admitted to an art exhibit at the Boston Athenaeum, Sarah Hale took the occasion to call the exhibition to her readers' attention. Sarah Freeman Clarke, the first Boston woman noted for landscape painting, wrote: "In 1827, I think, the first Athenaeum exhibition of pictures was announced. A joyous whisper went about that ladies might go to this exhibition unattended by a gentleman. Advanced womanhood will smile at this concession, granted by I know not what social power."

In 1833 Sarah Hale questioned, in print, why women were not invited to meet the president of the United States on his stay in Boston.

After nearly ten years as editor in Boston, she remarked on the "great change" in public opinion "respecting the estimation in which the influence of woman should be held. . . . The vast *moral power* of the sex, and the advantages which society will gain by having this power used wisely, is rapidly attracting the attention of philosophers as well as Christians—and statesmen and legislators cannot long neglect to make special provision for the education of females. And when woman enjoys the advantages of education in the manner appropriate to her character and duties, proportionally with man, she will no longer deserve or incur from him the epithet of 'romantic animal.' "

11

A Healthy Body

Women were said to be in better circumstances in the United States than in any other country. Perhaps, Sarah Hale conceded, but this was no reason to be complacent. Much more needed to be and could be done. And she was specific, "It has long seemed to us an imperative duty to train every female to the important art of attending the sick." Among her reasons was one that would certainly be challenged today: that was that women would perform this humble task more cheaply! The main thing, she felt then, was to get a foot in the door.

Sarah Hale went on to cite the endurance of women—at a time when popular belief said they were weak, sickly, and when it was the fashion for women to look pale as white daisies. For centuries the home care of the sick had fallen to women; why not then give them the information and training they needed to perform the best possible job, for their own families and for others. Sarah quoted reputable, renowned medical men and reviewed books giving the best, up-to-date information in this field. *The House I Live In*, by William A. Alcott, published in 1834, gave detailed anatomical and physiological information about the human body, with illustrations. Sarah Hale published extracts and even some of the drawings from this book in her *American Ladies'*

Magazine, so that readers could get a clear idea of what the book had to offer. Few books today are given review coverage like that—four pages in an important periodical.

When the young Englishwoman, Elizabeth Blackwell, was applying to study medicine in American colleges and being turned down by nearly every reputable college, she was supported in the *Lady's Book*. Even Sarah's friend, Dr. Oliver Wendell Holmes, then professor of anatomy and physiology at Harvard Medical School, was persuaded that women of serious purpose should at least be allowed to listen to lectures on medicine. Harriot Keziah Hunt, the first Boston woman to try to pursue a career in medicine, applied to Holmes for permission to attend lectures at Harvard in 1847, but, according to report, students overruled the faculty decision in her favor!

The reverse was the case when Miss Blackwell applied for admission to Geneva College in New York State. There the students approved of her coming, believing a spoof was being played on them by a rival school. They determined to call the bluff. Imagine their faces when the gentle young Miss Blackwell appeared in their lecture hall.

Nevertheless, she won their respect, gained practical experience with patients at the Philadelphia Hospital in the summer of 1848, and the next year received her medical degree from Geneva College—an honor to the college! The following spring when she toured London's principal medical institutions and hospitals, she must have startled the distinguished medical faculties when she appeared. She wore a "modest crinoline with pale blue frills, and flowers in her hair." She was petite and looked very happy at being treated as a celebrity.

A year later Sarah Hale was already advocating another new idea. On November 12, 1851, to complement the work of men missionaries in foreign lands, she organized the Ladies' Medical Missionary Society of Philadelphia. It had as its board of managers women from all the major sects, including the Friends and the Dutch Reformed Church. It was to reach out to the women in India, China, Turkey—wherever such missionaries would be accepted—to distribute information on female health, to educate women and their children in hygiene, and to open their minds to greater freedom of opportunity.

At a time when childbirth was often fatal, the topic of women's hygiene was considered highly indelicate. "Women prefer to suffer the extremity of danger and pain rather than waive those scruples of delicacy which prevent their maladies from being fully explored," admitted a professor of Jefferson College in Philadelphia.

In 1850 the Female Medical College of Philadelphia opened, despite prejudice and professional hostility, and forty women students enrolled. It was the world's first chartered medical school for women. And in Boston that same year the Female Medical Education Society was incorporated. Ten years later Sarah Hale noted that the medical colleges for women in Pennsylvania and New England were unique to the United States; no other country was known to have such colleges.

Not long after the first medical school for women opened, Marie Zakrzewska came to the United States from Germany. When very young she had assisted her mother at the school for midwives in Berlin. Filled with the desire to study medicine after graduating from that school, she heard of the Female Medical College in Philadelphia and with her sister came to America—hopefully to practice medicine. Marie eventually came under the patronage of the Blackwell sisters and joined them in soliciting funds for a New York Infirmary for Women and Children, which opened May 1, 1857, the first in the United States to be staffed entirely by women.

Although several of Sarah J. Hale's protégées graduated from the college in Philadelphia, and were ready to set sail as medical missionaries, they found the way blocked. Church authorities frowned on single women going out into the unknown to practice medicine and refused to sponsor them unless they were married to a missionary. Impasse. Still the society's training program went on, and eventually, not without some polite persuasion from Sarah Hale, the Board of the Methodist Church agreed to let Clara A. Swain "go out in a missionary capacity to the Women of the East." This was (1869) sixteen years after the first two young women were ready. Eighteen months later Mrs. Hale reported the opening of a women's hospital in India—the outcome of Miss Swain's and the society's sustained effort. So, almost imperceptibly and with infinite patience on the part of its supporters, the taboos were lifted, and age-old customs began to yield to the advantages of modern medicine and modern living.

Sarah Hale wrote, in March, 1852, "The whole human race will be benefited when woman enters on *her duties in her own sphere* as physician for her own sex and for children."

Now women from the Far East and from all countries of the world come to America to study in its colleges, just as American girls go abroad to study and work where their interests lead them.

As Sarah was reading through the medical journals in the late 1840s she must have started at a familiar name—William Thomas Morton. She had known him in Boston, where in his late teens he had worked as a clerk. Now he was making medical history by being the first to demonstrate the use of ether as a general anesthetic at Massachusetts General Hospital. It was October 16, 1846, when he gave the demonstration. But, as often happens, other scientists had been studying and experimenting with pain killers. As a result Dr. Morton became embroiled in a controversy over a prize for his work; at the same time the use of anesthesia in obstetrics had provoked a religious dispute.

Then Sarah Hale decided that she could not let a man whom she knew to be honest and trustworthy suffer. Taking up her pen, she wrote for the *Lady's Book* of March, 1853, "an accurate sketch of one whose name will, unquestionably, go down to posterity among the benefactors of mankind . . . Women even more than men should feel and express gratitude to the discoverer of a pain neutralizer, for on us falls the heaviest amount of physical suffering. . . . We have some personal knowledge of Dr. Morton, when as a mere youth he was struggling to educate and support himself. . . ." She gave the details of his education in dental surgery at the Massachusetts Medical College and elsewhere, to refute the charge that he was not scientifically educated. Of course, it was only after an award from Congress had been proposed—$100,000 to the pioneering doctor—that Dr. Morton was surrounded by suspicion, controversy, and counterclaims. As Sarah Hale pointed out to her readers, not until the award was offered did any rival or counterclaim appear. Congress never made the award. And Dr. Morton "in consequence of the interruption of his regular practice resulting from his efforts and experiments in establishing this great truth became poor in a cause which has made the world his debtor."

Sarah Hale's defense of Morton brought his plight to the attention of Godey's *Book's* many readers and helped to balance the scales in his favor.

William Thomas Morton died in poverty in New York City in 1868. In 1920 he was elected to the Hall of Fame.

12

Inequities or Iniquities?

"The term 'rights of woman' is one to which I have an almost constitutional aversion," Sarah Hale wrote in 1833. While campaigning for woman's greater freedom through education, she feared that women would alienate men by becoming demanding and domineering and "lose the attractions of the woman in the pedantry and affectation of the scholar." She hoped that men would eventually "be convinced that knowledge not only adds to woman's ability for usefulness, but to her power of pleasing; and that intellectual cultivation gives new charms to beauty, new loveliness to grace."

Some fifteen years later a Women's Rights Convention, the first in the United States, was held in Seneca Falls, New York, under the leadership of Elizabeth Cady Stanton, Lucretia Mott, and their friends, among whom was the abolitionist leader and former slave, Frederick Douglass. The public was shocked by their forthright Declaration of Sentiments asking for equality for women and for the women's right to vote. No attention was given to this convention as such in Godey's *Lady's Book* except for an editorial in December, which touched the subject obliquely. The editor cited the influence the magazine had had on public opinion as regards woman's sphere. "As the organ of this progress" the *Lady's Book* "is still ready to lead. . . . But softly . . ."

"We have said little of the Rights of Woman," wrote Sarah Hale in 1850, "but her first right is to education in its widest sense, to such education as will give her the full development of all her personal, mental and moral qualities. Having that, there will be no longer any question about her rights; and rights are liable to be perverted to wrongs when we are incapable of rightly exercising them. . . ." Reminding her readers that the *Lady's Book* had been "the first avowed advocate of the holy cause of woman's intellectual progress," she said, "We intend to go on . . . till our grand aim is accomplished, till female education shall receive the same careful attention and liberal support from public legislation as are bestowed on that of the other sex."

Even to ask for legislation for this purpose was a bold step at that time. Women had to think carefully before openly taking a public stand on the issue. Even one of the Blackwells admitted to watching herself and her friends to see if she were losing her femininity in asserting her rights. Other women feared to lose as much as they would gain by adopting the Women's Rights platform.

In 1848, at election time, the editor had announced that while men are engaged in the excitement of the electoral process, women do have a role. Each one must choose "a part to perform in the great movement of the age . . . and in what manner she can do the most good and promote greatest happiness. Study your own nature and constitution," she advised. "Learn the natural laws of health in order to be able to take care of yourself and others."

There was no question that the home and the education of her children was woman's domain, and Sarah Hale felt that women had more than enough to do in this area of activity. A typical Hale editorial on the subject, written in 1846, reads: "Remember that woman must *influence* while man *governs*, and that their duties, though equal in dignity and importance, can never be *identical*. Like the influence of the sun and air on the plant, both must unite in perfecting society; and which is of paramount value, can never be settled." She often reviewed current books on the subject, one of which, *The Legal Rights, Liabilities, etc. of Women*, by Edward D. Mansfield, she used as a frequent reference. As its title indicates, Mansfield's book dealt in detail with the legal rights of women from earliest times, with particular attention to their status in America as the law then (1845) provided. It was granted that women were citizens, but without the right to vote. According to Scriptural and civil law, husband and wife were considered one person; the husband had the right to speak for his wife and the wife's personal property became his on their marriage.

According to Edward Mansfield's book, a wife's rights included protection, maintenance, and "necessaries" (food, clothing, and medicine) suitable to her condition in life. Only by a settlement arranged prior to the marriage and by bequests in trust to her separate use, might the wife control some property.

In *Manners* Sarah Hale wrote, "I place woman's office above man's because moral influence is superior to mechanical invention. *Man is greater than his work*; and women's mission is to mould mind, and form character; while man's work deals with material things, both equally need the cultivation of their intellectual powers to fit them for their duties."

She cited the statistics on divorce in Massachusetts and noted the laxity of the laws and the need for mutual consideration between marriage partners.

Making a comfortable and agreeable home was a vocation not to be deprecated. "Character," Sarah Hale wrote,". . . is as clearly displayed in the arrangements and adornments of a house as in any other way. Who cannot read grace, delicacy, and refinement in the lady of a house, simply by looking at the little elegances and beauties with which she has surrounded herself in her home? Nor are large sums necessary to produce this effect. . . ."

All of this sounded too soft to Elizabeth Cady Stanton and other feminists, but when it came to woman's right to use and protect her property, Sarah Hale was in the front ranks of battle. Having been a widow without financial resources gave her the keenest appreciation of women's need to hold onto what little they earned. In 1837 she had tackled the thorny subject of "The Rights of Married Women" in a five-column article. Like many others, she was pleased when, in April 1848, the Married Women's Property Bill was passed in New York State. This enabled women to own real estate.

She led off the year 1856 with an editorial about a woman writer in England separated from her husband, who was persecuting her by cutting off all funds, even her earnings from her own writing! "Partly to illustrate the blessings we American women enjoy under our better system of laws and usages, and partly to awaken public attention to the still existing defects in our own institutions, we show a glimpse of married life in England."

Caroline Norton, the woman in question, had published a pamphlet stating, "I cannot divorce my husband either for adultery, desertion, or cruelty; I *must* remain married to his name. I am . . . in a worse position than if I had been divorced by him. . . . I do not receive, and have not received for the last three years, a single farthing from my husband. He retains, and always has retained property that was left in my home, gifts made to me by my own family on my marriage, and to my mother, articles bought from my literary earnings, &c. He receives from my trustees the interest of the portion bequeathed to me by my father. . . . I have also (as Mr. Norton impressed on me by subpoenaing my publishers) the power of earning by literature, which fund, though it be the grant of Heaven, not the legacy of earth, is no more legally mine than my family property. When we first separated, he offered me, as sole provision, a small pension paid by government to each of my father's children, reckoning that pension as *his*. . . . In 1851, my mother died; she left me (through my brother, to guard it from my husband) a small annuity as an addition to my income. Mr. Norton first endeavored to claim her legacy, and then balanced the first payment under her will by arbitrarily stopping my allowance. I insisted that the allowance was secured by her own signature and other signatures to a formal deed; he defied me to prove it, as by law man and wife were one, and could not contract with each other, and the deed was, therefore, good for nothing."

In an article in the *North British Review*, a reviewer, a man and presumably one versed in the laws, acknowledged that this was an example of "inconceivable injustice. . . . there are cases . . . where the legal non-existence of the wife is as revolting to the reason as to the feelings. . . . As the English law now stands, a husband may claim from the employer of his discarded wife all the money that she has earned; and the employer is bound to give it to him. Any contract entered into with *her* is mere waste paper; she may earn money for her husband, as his horse or his ox may earn it for him, but not for herself. If she has been permitted to receive her earnings, and has contrived by painful economy and self-denial to save any portion of them, she cannot leave her savings after her death even to her own children; they are absolutely her husband's, and he may take them and give all to the children of a paramour, or squander them upon the paramour herself. . . ." The review concluded: "we could not . . . maintain a law in its operation more flagrantly unjust. . . .

"This theory of the non-existence of women pursues its victims from the school-room to the grave. . . . Single women are legally capable of independent action; but they are seldom or never educated for it. . . . If they continue in their singleness, having been educated for non-existence, they are incapable of acting for themselves; they are fit, indeed, only to be absorbed."

In her column Sarah Hale outlined "What Is Needed in America." It was no less than a plea for "the Honorable Senate and House of Representatives in Congress assembled" to set aside three or four million acres of public land "to endow at least one Normal School in every State for the gratuitous education of female teachers." After all, "the standard of woman is the moral thermometer of the nation," she said, and "no public provision has been made, no college or university endowed where young women may have similar advantages of instruction now open to *young men* in every State of the Union."

13

Marriages and a Festival

While she was devoting countless hours to reading, editing, and planning articles and stories for the magazine—and writing them, too—Sarah's daughters were finishing their schooling and finding their futures. Both had trained at Emma Willard's Female Seminary in Troy, New York.

Emma Willard, whom Sarah met first in Boston, had played a pioneer's role in demanding the training of women as teachers. The Willard Association for the Mutual Improvement of Female Teachers (founded in 1837 as an alumnae group) was the first to bring this need to public attention. Emma Willard asked Sarah Hale and Lydia Sigourney to be honorary vice-presidents of this association.

Although the Willard School was one of the first in the country to train women to teach, it did not overlook the likelihood that its students would at some time become wives and mothers. Therefore, the management of a household and the early education of children were also part of the curriculum. As if to exemplify this, Frances Ann and Sarah Josepha Hale took separate paths after graduation.

In 1844 Frances Ann married a young naval surgeon, Dr. Lewis Boudinot Hunter, of Princeton and Philadelphia, while her sister became a schoolteacher. Sarah Josepha taught in Georgia for a number of years before returning to Philadelphia to teach. Her brother William also taught school, in Richmond, Virginia, after graduation from Harvard College in 1842. From his training in civil engineering, he turned to the study of law and was admitted to the Texas bar in 1846. Soon after he set up a law partnership with a cousin in Galveston in the new state of Texas.

There was great rejoicing in the Hale family when Horatio returned from his five-year absence. He had traveled via a Hudson's Bay Company ship to Mexico, then overland alone to Vera Cruz and so north into the interior, arriving home in May 1842, full of stories of the wonders he had seen. His reports of the land areas on the West Coast were helpful later in the dispute between the United States and Great Britain over the Oregon boundary.

His next important task was to set down his scientific findings for the U.S. Exploring Expedition. Here his mother's guidance in the preparation of the manuscript for the press was invaluable, and Horatio's volume VI of the official record of the Wilkes expedition was completed in remarkably short time. Published in 1846, it comprised 665 pages on the *Ethnography and Philology of the U.S. Exploring Expedition.* It was the first published report of the scientists on the expedition, the whole report not being completed for some years. It won much praise; colleagues stated later (in the Royal Society of Canada's Proceedings for 1897) that Hale's "classifications and investigations have stood the test of all later inquiries, and, as we grow familiar with the subjects treated by him, we become more and more forcibly impressed by the keen insight into the structure of language. . . . The results and method that he pursued are the more admirable when we consider how few the advantages were that the young Harvard student enjoyed in those times in this line of research, and that the methods of investigating primitive languages were to a great extent his own creation. . . . Many are his contributions to science, and they rank among the best work done in America."

His writing and editing done, Horatio departed for several years of study and travel in Europe.

His mother was content to visit New England. Sarah J. Hale had not seen her native village for many years, but she was invited in 1846 to attend the Fourth of July celebration in her birthplace, Newport, New Hampshire. It was also the eightieth anniversary of the founding of the town by settlers from Connecticut, among them Sarah's father. She resolved to go, taking "the cars" (railroad) for as much of the 400-mile journey as possible. It was a brief period of relaxation.

Coming directly "from the level country of the Delaware where the city of straight streets lies flat and even as the waters of a sleeping lake," Sarah found "the magnificence of these mountain views . . . most strikingly impressive." After so many years there was not a relative to welcome her and only a few early associates, "yet it was home still." The railroad (from Lowell, Massachusetts, to Concord, New Hampshire) was "the pleasantest we ever traveled" and from it she viewed "the new manufacturing towns at short intervals."

The Fourth of July celebration in the small mountain village might seem old-fashioned now, but it was typical of the festivities held in towns throughout New England at that time. The Declaration of Independence, then papers on the town history were read to the assembled spectators. And, after a "good and abundant feast," a hymn was deaconed after the old style, a line at a time, to the tune of "Old Hundred." Sarah Hale had written this hymn, called "Gathering Song," for the occasion:

> How blest to find a resting-place,
> A gathering goal in life's swift race,

Where hands that Time has long untwined,
Once more in friendly clasp are joined.

Though parted from our place of birth,
Yet still, like flower seeds left in earth,
Its deep remembrances remain,
And, waked to life, unfold again.

And thus, with hearts in bloom, we come,
From many a dear and distant home,
Like pilgrims to their own roof-tree,
To keep this day of jubilee.

And though a shade of sadness fall,
That come who may, they come not all,
Yet Love shall here his torch renew,
And Hope, assured, look upward too.

And while with grateful hearts we say
The God of old is ours to-day,
The same who led our fathers on
Till freedom's heritage was won,

Still onward leads, while blessings flow
As Heaven had turned its tide below,
Oh, may each voice and spirit free
Bless God for this sweet jubilee!

The editor of Godey's *Book* invited "the people of other towns to follow this mode of keeping the national jubilee . . . the people of Newport, N.H., have been the first, we think, to set the fashion of an 'Historical Celebration.' " Another national festival in which she was much interested was Thanksgiving Day. She was already campaigning for greater *national* unity.

Then Sarah added a semihumorous report of her return journey. How hard it must have been to turn her back on the mountains and return to the "city of straight streets"! Because "for the last eight years we had only traveled by steam," she decided to take the old-fashioned stagecoach from Newport to Boston; they were still to be found in the old Granite State. And a long and roundabout journey it was, the moral of which was: "The lady who travels in a stagecoach unattended should always get out when the stage stops and look after her trunk." Hers was missing for three days!

Sarah's youngest son, William, became "renowned for his handling of the old Spanish claims which immediately flooded the courts of Texas upon its separation from Mexico." It has been said that "no complete history of Texas can be written without mention of William Hale."

By 1855 both sons were married and Horatio was living in Canada, but there were visits from time to time—and of course family correspondence. Both daughters continued to live near their mother's home.

In 1856 her daughter, Sarah, opened her own private school on Rittenhouse Square in Philadelphia. In January, 1861, this advertisement appeared in Godey's *Lady's Book*:

Miss S. J. Hale's Boarding and Day School for Young Ladies, 1826 Rittenhouse Square, Philadelphia.

This school is designed to give a thorough and liberal English education, to furnish the best facilities for acquiring the French language, and the best instruction in music and the other accomplishments. An accomplished French teacher resides in the family, and also an excellent teacher of music, who gives her personal attention to pupils while practising. The moral training and the health and physical development of the scholars are carefully attended to.

References: Mrs. Emma Willard, Troy, N. Y.; Henry Vethake, LLD., Wm. B. Stevens, D.D., Wm. H. Ashhurst, Esq., Louis A. Godey, Esq., Philadelphia; Charles Hodge, D.D., Princeton, N. J.; and others.

Sarah was happy watching her Hunter grandchildren grow up. One of her letters mentions "a dear little black-eyed baby with hair like a raven's wing. . . . It looks so nearly as my babies did that it seems almost my own." She especially enjoyed choosing books for her grandchildren. She admired the works of George MacDonald, Louisa May Alcott, and Susan Coolidge, among others. She wrote the following "Lines" in the album of a granddaughter:

> Never waste the morning
>   In your sleeping-room;
> Hark! the birds are singing,
>   Look! the roses bloom:
> Up and out to greet them
>   With a song of praise;
> 'Tis a thankful spirit
>   Makes our happy days.
>
> Childhood is the morning
>   Of our human day;
> With the reason's dawning
>   We should learn to pray
> For the faith that brightens
>   As our years increase;
> Then life's evening shadows
>   Will bear the bow of peace.

(February 5, 1859)

14

Peaks and Valleys of Popularity

From time to time publisher Godey reported on the increasing numbers of readers. "From Maine to the Rocky Mountains there is scarcely a hamlet, however inconsiderable, where it [the *Lady's Book*] is not received and read; and in the larger towns and cities it is universally distributed," he declared in December 1841.

From a literary standpoint the best years of Godey's *Book* were between 1837 and 1850. The most productive and popular fiction writers regularly contributed and articles were often "expressly written for the *Lady's Book.*"

A series by Edgar Allan Poe on the New York literati caused particular excitement. Writers, both men and women, who made their headquarters in New York, were discussed with rare frankness. Poe, then thirty-seven years old, was himself a well-known writer in both the United States and Europe, some of his work having found its way to England and the Continent. He had made enemies as well as friends, as those in the public eye will. Because Poe was a somewhat controversial figure and because of the stature of Godey's *Book*, in which his articles appeared, the series made a greater sensation than expected. Poe's personal acquaintance with the subjects gave it added interest.

Today the "Literati" articles seem mildly derogatory in some cases; they are uneven, "hastily done," as Poe was

frank to state, and meant to raise the hackles of his less
favorite subjects. Naturally, the writers themselves were
agog to see what Poe had said about them.

From the first article Poe wrote for the series he promised
frank opinions regarding the leading writers of the
day—comments such as colleagues and peers would give, not
"the quackery," as Poe called it, which usually appeared in
the press. He praised Hawthorne's work as that of an "extraordinary genius," although "his walk is limited."
Longfellow was favored by his position "as a man of
property and a professor at Harvard," but, Poe said, he was
regarded as "a determined imitator and a dexterous adapter
of the ideas of other people." Poe claimed that Longfellow
had plagiarized his own "Haunted Palace" poem.

Of Lydia Maria Child, poet, novelist, and abolitionist, he
said: "Some of her magazine papers are distinguished for
graceful and brilliant *imagination*—a quality rarely noticed
in our countrywomen." He then went on to describe her
appearance, a novel feature in literary columns: "Her dress is
usually plain, not even neat—anything but fashionable. Her
bearing needs excitement to impress it with life and dignity.
She is of that order of beings who are themselves only on
'great occasions.' . . . I need scarcely add that she has
always been distinguished for her energetic and active
philanthropy."

However Lydia Child may have felt about these comments, Poe treated most of the women writers with some
delicacy and on the whole favorably. The men, especially
those whose weaknesses he knew, fared less well. His close-
to-libelous attack on Thomas Dunn English seems un-
necessarily cruel and unworthy. As might have been expected, English, a professional man (lawyer and poet and
eventually a congressman), retaliated . . . and not only in
print. When Poe came to see him with an apology and, at the

same time, seeking a favor, he refused, and Poe was turned out of English's office with blows. Poe sued the New York *Mirror* (in which English's printed reply had appeared) for libel, and when the case came to trial in February 1847 he received $225 in damages and costs, a total of $492. By his injudicious remarks, however, Poe had gained nothing and lost much. The controversy proved unpleasant for both parties and was damaging to Poe's reputation.

The first installment of "Literati" in Godey's *Book* was completely sold out and had to be reprinted quickly to supply the demand. Godey was probably pleased with the rush of business, but the magazine was besieged by letters of protest, too, and threats to cancel subscriptions. When the June issue appeared, with a reprint of the first "Literati" article, in response to demand, the publisher added the following statement:

> The Authors and Mr. Poe.—We have received several letters from New York anonymously and from personal friends requesting us to be careful what we allow Mr. Poe to say of New York authors, many of whom are our personal friends. We reply to one and all that we have nothing to do but publish Mr. Poe's opinions, *not our own.* Whether we agree with Mr. Poe or not is another matter. We are not to be intimidated by a threat of a loss of friends. The May edition was exhausted the first of May and we have had orders for hundreds from Boston and New York which we could not supply. This first number of the series is republished in this number which also contains No. 2.
>
> Many attempts have been made and are making to forestall public opinion . . . others are busy with reports of Mr. Poe's illness. Mr. Poe has been ill,

> but we have letters from him of very recent date, also a new batch of Literati, which show anything but feebleness of body or mind."

This statement has in it the intrepid ring of Sarah Hale's style, and it is possible that she and the publisher collaborated.

In November 1846 Poe's story, "The Cask of Amontillado," appeared in the *Book*. A year later Godey's *Book* published Poe's essay on Hawthorne, and in 1849 several little-known pieces. Poe's health, however, was rapidly deteriorating. With the death of his wife Virginia on January 29, 1847, at the cottage in Fordham, New York, Poe's demons—including poverty—took hold of him with redoubled force. He died October 7, 1849.

Godey's editor wrote these words for the January, 1850, issue:

> The Late Edgar A. Poe—The December number of the *Book* contained some amusing specimens of American poets; and among them one of the poetry of the late Mr. Poe. Lest some of our readers should suppose that we had been trifling with the memory of a gifted but unfortunate son of genius, we deem it proper to state that the article had been sent to the press before the lamented death of the poet occurred; otherwise it would not have been inserted.

Sarah Hale could not bear readers to think that Poe's light verses (written when he was close to starvation, although they could not know that) had been published frivolously or unfeelingly. With this note she proved again that she did care. Poe's verses in question contained these stanzas, written with sad irony:

Then old Mistress Hubbard,
   Felt pity herself;
She opened the cupboard,
   She looked on the shelf,
Adown-board and up-board,
   And back of the delf;
She searched the whole cupboard,
   Each corner and shelf.

. . .

And she said: "Broken-hearted
   And bone-wanting one!
The truth is imparted,
   The cupboard has none:
The gold chain has parted,
   Sinks gloomy the sun;
The bones have departed!
   The deed has been done!

Poe's connections with Louis Godey and Sarah Hale were vitually the only ones of his many professional contacts that remained harmonious to the end—largely due to "the patience, tact, and sympathetic comprehension of the woman who was the *Book's* wise editor" as Ruth Finley commented in *The Lady of Godey's.*

Mrs. Hale often reiterated her aim as editor, "to subserve the best interests of women," and in 1850 she noted the "wonderful changes" in public opinion that had occurred since the first issue of the magazine. In this year a new series of quotations on the condition and situation of women began in the Editor's Table. She called attention to:

the Homestead Laws, and the security given that the property of the married woman shall remain in her own possession . . . the efforts made to open new channels of industry and profitable professions for those women who have to support themselves are deserving of much praise; but, she persevered, Government, national or state, has never yet provided suitably for the education of women. Girls, as well as boys, have the advantages of the free school system; but no public provision has been made, no college or university endowed where young women may have similar advantages of instruction now open to young men in every State of the Union. . .

Holding these sentiments, our "Book" has never swerved from its straightforward course of aiding women to improve themselves, while it has aimed to arouse public sentiment to help onward this improvement. For this, we keep domestic virtues and home duties before our readers, we give patterns and directions for feminine employments, we show the benefits of female education, and for this we have *twice* brought before Congress our petition for aid; and now we come the *third* time.

Then she offered a Memorial to "the Honorable Senate and House of Representatives in Congress assembled," asking them to set apart "three or four million of acres of the public national domains" to endow "at least one *Normal School* in every State for the gratuitous education of female teachers."

During these same busy years she was also compiling material for a publication that would be a more enduring accomplishment than her oft-quoted children's verse. It occupied several years of writing, editing, and correspondence. Symbolizing her dedication to the cause of women,

Woman's Record is a 918-page collection of "Sketches of all the distinguished women from the Creation to A.D. 1850," with 230 portraits and samples of their written work, arranged in Four Eras. Even the feminists of her day who criticized her adversely had to admit that this was "a labor for which our sex owes her a debt of gratitude. . . . To exhume nearly seventeen hundred women from oblivion, classify them, and set forth their distinguished traits of character, was indeed a herculean labor. This is a valuable book of reference for the girls of to-day. When our opponents depreciate the achievements of woman they can turn to the *Woman's Record* and find grand examples of all the cardinal virtues, of success in art, science, literature, and government." "The *Record*," said John S. Hart, a distinguished educator and critic, in *The Female Prose Writers of America*, "will be enduring not only of woman in general but of the high aims, the indefatigable industry, the varied reading, and just discrimination of its ever to be honoured author."

In her remarks on the Fourth Era, the most recent in *Woman's Record*, Sarah Hale said "a subtle device of evil has been to keep women in restraint and concealment. It is unfeminine even to express openly their abhorrence of sin. And if they seek to do good, it must be by stealth. . . . Every false religion [i.e. philosophy or doctrine] may be known by this—it represents woman as *inferior* to man, it sacrifices her honor, happiness, and glory to his brute appetites, sensuous passions and selfish pride. In such an atmosphere, the animal lives, the angel perishes, till humanity is morally dead." This is a strong statement for her, but it clearly shows her strengthening feeling for the equality of woman with man.

Woman's Record went into a third edition, of which Professor Hart wrote: "A third edition of a work of such magnitude as this, after so short a time . . . is no slight attestation to its solid value. Mrs. Hale has done for her sex what Dr. Allibone [compiler of Allibone's *Critical Dictionary of English Literature*] has done for British and American authors. By long years of patient and persistent labor and research, she has gathered the authentic evidences of what the eminent ones of her own sex, in all ages of the world, have been and have done, and has placed the fruits of her labors in this noble and enduring *Record*."

Continuing her deep and abiding interest in poetry, she also prepared *A Complete Dictionary of Poetical Quotations, containing Selections from the Writings of the Poets of England and America*, a volume of 600 double-column octavo pages. This predated Bartlett's *Familiar Quotations* by five years.

Sarah Hale also revised and enlarged a favorite selection, first put together in 1832, of flower poems called *Flora's Interpreter*, adding a section called "Fortuna Flora" on the mystical language of flowers. She placed special emphasis in this new edition on "the best specimens of American poetry," remarking that the earlier edition had been much imitated, "but we trust that in the part now added . . . no one will thus interfere, for some years at least, to take from us the profits of projecting and preparing a work that has cost us much time and research." But, she said, "we feel quite at liberty to select whatever is best and brightest from . . . British genius for this work, because *Flora's Interpreter* has been republished in London, and, under the title of *The Book of Flowers*, sold largely without any remuneration to the author. It is quite probable that this new and enlarged work may have the same honor." Again this refers to the lack of copyright law, but the editor here ignored the fact that American publishers had for many years reaped profits from the works of Scott, Dickens, Thackeray, and other popular British writers without compensating them.

About this time also, Godey's *Book* and Sarah Hale were publicizing the need to restore George Washington's former home, Mount Vernon, an enterprise to galvanize the nation's unity and patriotism. The editor could see some potentially dangerous rents in the nation's solidarity. She noted in 1850 that "while the ocean of political life is heaving and raging with the storm of partisan passions among the men of America, the women, the true conservators of peace and good-will, should be careful to cultivate every gentle feeling and give prominence to every public exhibition of patriotism." She quoted and praised Longfellow's patriotic poem, "The Building of the Ship."

Whenever she could discover a means to rally her readers behind the union of the states, Sarah made use of it. Serializing "Heroic Women of the Revolution," by Mrs. Elizabeth F. Ellet, reminded readers of the goals and sacrifices of the founders of the republic.

In 1856 Godey claimed 100,000 subscribers. More services were added to increase the magazine's usefulness. Plans for cottages, "a small villa," and other constructions were included, and the magazine undertook to obtain books for subscribers "who choose books that we notice." Listings and information on colleges and schools for young ladies continued to be published.

New, woman-saving inventions were applauded. For one, Masser's Self-Acting Patent Ice-cream freezer and beater made its appearance in 1850.

The editor of the *Lady's Book* not only welcomed labor-saving devices that would aid the homemaker, she encouraged their invention. All of this was founded on her belief in the importance of education in freeing women. "There can be no education without leisure, and without leisure education is worthless," she said.

When the sewing machine came on the market, she saw its ultimate result, the relief of thousands of women from the drudgery of handsewing what could be done more swiftly and efficiently by machine, and urged readers to use it.

In 1853 Sarah Hale invited inventors to put their minds to work to produce something that would help women with the family washing—a never-ending task. The following spring a queer-looking contraption was unveiled, the first practical washing machine! The crude drawing in the *Lady's Book* shows a handcranked model, using the principle of the lever. A woman could sit while turning it, and it saved her hands from the effects of harsh soap and water.

Every device that would lighten the tasks and ease the labors of woman was important to the editor of the *Lady's Book*, and she was willing to publicize them as soon as they proved their usefulness. Godey's also provided a consumer information or protection service with advice on the best sewing machine, piano, or other product.

By 1863, as the mass production of clothing began in the United States, the *Book* was showing dress models that could be bought ready-made.

Some years later the magazine published a fashion plate of the new "professional" woman with a typewriter made by W. H. Travis, Philadelphia—the lady's hand lightly touching the keys.

15

Gleams of Light in Darkness

Near the beginning of the Civil War, in October 1861, the Editor wrote: "While clouds and darkness overhang the land, we naturally welcome with double pleasure whatever promises permanent good for the future. The founding of an institution like Vassar Female College, in a year like the present, is a peculiarly cheering event." Sarah described the course of study proposed and congratulated the founder on initiating the program and overseeing it to insure that his wishes were carried out. "We have the satisfaction of knowing," she added, "that the founder and the other trustees of the college are sparing no pains to secure . . . such a staff of instructors as will render it most efficient for the purposes contemplated. It will be truly gratifying to all who have labored during the past years to promote the cause of female education to know that their work is about to find its crowning success in this noble institution."

Throughout its organization period Sarah Hale kept in touch with Matthew Vassar, giving his college-to-be priceless advance publicity and the benefit of her years of experience. Late in 1863 she learned that there were to be no women executives in the organization! Was this possible—for a women's college? She immediately dictated an editorial, taken down by her grandson, Richard Hunter, who was helping her during a time when she had eye trouble: Vassar

College had "one defect and this may be easily amend-ed"—again a tactful way of putting it. She was assured that Mr. Vassar would put the situation right as soon as he could. By June 1864, Sarah had another editorial ready, no action having been taken at Vassar. The war, of course, and some opposition or misunderstanding on Vassar's Board of Trustees had caused delay. The college, scheduled to open in 1864 (ground for the first building had been broken on July 4, 1861), did not, in fact, open its doors until 1865. Meanwhile, Mrs. Hale was bringing all her powers of persuasion to bear to insure that this college, which might be a model for similar institutions in the future, would have representative women in executive posts. The final roster of officers included Hannah W. Lyman as principal; Maria Mitchell, the astronomer from Nantucket, who in 1848 was unanimously elected an honorary member of the American Academy of Arts and Sciences; Alida C. Avery, M.D., a woman resident physician and professor of physiology and hygiene; Delia F. Woods, instructor of physical education; and eighteen women "under instructors," or a total of twenty-two women and eight men on the faculty.

Sarah's effort to have Vassar College offer a course in domestic science, a phrase that she coined early in her career, did not succeed. For some reason Vassar's board of trustees would not approve this.

One more defect remained to be corrected, the name of the college. For years, as an editor, Sarah Hale had opposed the use of the word "female" to indicate human beings. In the *Lady's Book* she had emphasized what were then considered the proper terms for women in the professions—authoress, editress, sculptress, and so forth. In Grammatical Errors, August 1857, she again called attention to the improper use of the word "female"—as in "female nurses," or "female colleges." She advised, "when reading draw your pencil through this word whenever it occurs as the substitute for girl, woman, lady, etc." To use it in referring to a college is an "absurdity," she said. Now she wanted to be sure that Vassar would never be embarrassed by having the incorrect usage on the front of its building or on its letterheads, to be haunted by it for years to come. "Why degrade the feminine sex to the level of animals?" she asked Mr. Vassar. ". . . I write thus earnestly because I wish to have Vassar College take the lead in this great improvement in our language. . . . Pray do not, my good friend, disappoint me. . . . I plead for the good of Vassar College, for the honor of womanhood and the glory of God.—Truly your friend, Sarah Josepha Hale." Matthew Vassar wrote on June 27, 1866, to tell Mrs. Hale that the offending word would be excised; and it was crossed off of that very piece of stationery and expunged from the front of the college building.

For six or seven of Vassar's crucial beginning years, Mrs. Hale and Godey's *Book* watched over and sought to promote this college, which was designed to provide women with as good an education as men had been getting for so many years.

Another objective came to fruition during the war—and perhaps because of it. For twenty years "one of the strongest wishes of my heart," Sarah said, was to make Thanksgiving a national holiday—the last Thursday of November.

In her novel, *Northwood*, she had proposed an annual offering on Thanksgiving Day from each of America's 40,000 churches to free the slaves, until "finally, every obstacle to the *real freedom* of America would be melted away. . . ." Thus, so long ago, she had implied that America could not be fully free until there was no slavery within its borders.

Thanksgiving, as a time for family reunions and rejoicing in the harvests of a bountiful land, had been extolled in many poems and in fiction. It was one of the first holidays not disapproved by the Puritan forefathers. More often, in the first winters of the 1620s, it was a day of fast and thanksgiving, rather than of feasting. As one of his earliest official acts, George Washington proclaimed November 26, 1789, a day of national thanksgiving. He, too, hoped such a day of quiet, prayerful thought would help to unite the new country under its recently ratified Constitution.

But Thanksgiving was not celebrated in every state, or even on the same days in the various states, until 1863. Some towns were as late as the first or second Thursday in December in celebrating it. And in the South even Sarah's relatives were divided in celebrating Thanksgiving, for it was considered a *Northern* holiday.

As the country grew more divided over the issue of slavery, Sarah Hale pondered what would hold the Union together. With the *Lady's Book* as a platform, she could exert considerable influence over a national audience—as she had for other causes. These United States had much to be thankful for, and she would tell her readers so. She wrote, and she wrote, and she wrote, not only editorials, but personal letters appealing to the governors of all the states and territories, to the presidents, from Buchanan to Lincoln, and to influential persons of her own acquaintance. Gradually, response to her appeals grew until by 1852, twenty-nine states and all the territories united on the date of the festival. Mrs. Hale emphasized the fourth Thursday in November as the ideal date because it was the one Washington himself had chosen. Thousands of letters went forth from her desk—handwritten, of course, by herself or an assistant, for there were as yet no typewriters or duplicating machines—all advocating the adoption of Thanksgiving as a national holiday on the fourth Thursday in November.

A Thanksgiving dinner as it was then served in New England is described in *Northwood*:

> A long table, formed by placing two of the ordinary size together, was set forth in the parlor; . . . The

table covered with a damask cloth, vieing in whiteness and nearly equaling in texture the finest imported, though spun, woven and bleached by Mrs. Romilly's own hand, was now intended for the whole household, every child having a seat on this occasion; and the more the better, it being considered an honor for a man to sit down to his Thanksgiving dinner surrounded by a large family. The provision is always sufficient for a multitude, every farmer in the country being at this season plentifully supplied, and every one proud of displaying his abundance and prosperity.

The roasted turkey took precedence on this occasion . . . sending forth the rich odor of its savory stuffing, and finely covered with the froth of the basting. At the foot of the board a sirloin of beef, flanked on either side by a leg of pork and loin of mutton, seemed placed as a bastion to defend innumerable bowls of gravy and plates of vegetables disposed in that quarter. A goose and pair of ducklings occupied side stations on the table, the middle being graced, as always . . . by that rich burgomaster . . . a chicken pie. This pie . . . enriched and seasoned with a profusion of butter and pepper, and covered with an excellent puff paste, is, like the celebrated pumpkin pie, an indispensable part of a good and true Yankee Thanksgiving . . .

Plates of pickles, preserves, and butter [and all the necessary seasonings] left hardly sufficient room for the plates of the company, a wine glass and two tumblers . . .

There was a huge plum pudding, custards and pies of every name and description ever known in Yankee land; yet the pumpkin pie occupied the most distinguished niche. There were also several kinds of rich cake, and a variety of sweetmeats and fruits. On the sideboard was ranged a goodly number of decanters and bottles; the former filled with currant wine, and the latter with excellent cider and ginger beer—a beverage Mrs. Romilly prided herself on preparing in perfection.

[Once the family was stationed around the table the father asked a blessing, which] was not merely a form of words . . . It was the breathings of a good and grateful heart acknowledging the mercies received, and sincerely thanking the Giver of every good gift for the plenteous portion he had bestowed.

The menu elsewhere was not always so traditional or so plentiful. One New Hampshire woman made her Thanksgiving mince pies one year with a filling of bear's meat and dried pumpkin, sweetened with maple sugar, under a cornmeal crust. Every family, of course, did not have that much with which to feast, so it became the custom to think of less provident or less fortunate neighbors and to send baskets of food to those who needed them.

A Bostonian recalled the thrill he felt as a boy at hearing the governor's Proclamation of Thanksgiving Day read in the Brattle Street Meeting-House and the announcement made that on the Sunday before a contribution would be taken for the poor. "Every human being went to 'meeting' on the morning of Thanksgiving Day," including this boy of four years.

He also recalled the Thanksgiving dinners. After eating as much as you could, "then you went to work on the fruits as you could. The use of dried fruits at the table was much more frequent in those days. Dates, prunes, raisins, figs, and nuts held a much more prominent place in a handsome dessert than they do now. Recollect that oranges were all brought from the West Indies or from the Mediterranean in sailing vessels, and were by no means served in the profusion with which they are served now." He recalled, too, with special feeling, a Marlborough pie, which was one of the specialties at Thanksgiving dinner, as "a sort of lemon pie," for which every good housekeeper thought she had a better recipe than anyone else.

The *Lady's Book*, in its culinary department, offered suggestions for alternate dishes: Soodjee, a fish delicacy; ham soaked in cider three weeks, stuffed with sweet potatoes and baked in maple syrup; Indian pudding and Frumenty Sauce—many of them seasoned with the good New England flavors the editor remembered.

As war became imminent, Sarah Hale urged that "as every state join in Union Thanksgiving on the 24th of this month [November 1859], would it not be a renewed pledge of love and loyalty to the Constitution of the United States which guarantees peace, prosperity, progress and perpetuity to our great Republic?"

She renewed her plea in 1861: "Yes, amidst all the agitations that stir the minds of men and cause the hearts of women to tremble . . . the mercy of the Lord is over all his children." While citing the plentiful harvests and freedom from pestilence and wasting sicknesses as cause for thanksgiving, she added, "would that we could add *peace has reigned, and good-will been extended*! but we must all acknowledge that the goodness of God has not failed. Shall we not, then, lay aside our enmities and strifes, and suspend our worldly cares, toils, and pursuits on *one day* in the year, devoting it to a public Thanksgiving for all the good gifts God has bestowed on us and on all the earth?"

What deep **satis**faction she felt, after all this effort, when, on October 3, **1863**, in the midst of the Civil War, Abraham Lincoln wrote the first national Thanksgiving Proclamation since Washington's time, appointing the last Thursday of November as the date. Lincoln's words were:

I do, therefore, invite my fellow-citizens in every part of the United States, and also those who are at sea and those who are sojourning in foreign lands, to set apart and observe the last Thursday of November next (November 26) as a day of thanksgiving and praise to our beneficent Father who dwelleth in the heavens. And I recommend to them that, while offering up the ascriptions justly due to Him for singular deliverances and blessings, they do also, with humble penitence for our national perverseness and disobedience, commend to His tender care all those who have become widows, orphans, mourners, or sufferers in the lamentable civil strife in which we are unavoidably engaged, and fervently implore the interposition of the almighty hand to heal the wounds of the nation, and to restore it, as soon as may be consistent with the Divine purposes, to the full enjoyment of peace, harmony, tranquillity, and union.

Sarah Hale brought the story up to date in her book *Manners* (1868):

Our late beloved and lamented President Lincoln recognized the truth of these ideas [about a national celebration] as soon as they were presented to him. His reply to our appeal was a proclamation, appointing Thursday, November 26, 1863, as the day of national Thanksgiving. But, at that time, and also in November, 1864, he was not able to influence the States in rebellion, so that the festival was necessarily incomplete.

Since the close of the war, these obstacles have been removed, and President Johnson's Proclamation for the National Thanksgiving on *the last Thursday of November*, 1866, was observed over all the country. Thus the family union of States and Territories in our Great Republic was fixed and hallowed by the people in the ninetieth year of American Independence.

16

The Storm and Its Aftermath

Citizens of all regions must make an effort to understand one another, Sarah Hale urged. "This union of hearts and memories . . . must preserve and perpetuate our political union," she editorialized in August 1845. "When feelings of kindly interest shall be cherished by all as sincerely as by that good New England mother and her son [in Kentucky], there will be no danger of discord between the states. The narrow spirit that sees a rival or enemy in every different section, will yield to the ties of relationship or good feeling, binding individuals and families to cherish and extend the familiarity of intercourse which may now be maintained with every part of our common country." A new Post Office law and the "power of steam" would bring the various parts of the country in closer, more frequent contact.

Women especially could foster friendships, bridging the gaps between the widely distant states so that "not a star will ever disappear from our banner, though its broad folds should in time cover and protect the whole Continent." This was written at the time of the annexation of Texas and as President Polk was attempting to buy or otherwise acquire California.

Under Godey's policy of "no politics," no direct reference to the great national division on slavery and to the eventual

Civil War could be made in the *Lady's Book*. Yet Sarah J. Hale was well aware of the division threatening the country. Her relatives, friends, and readers in every region could provide her with grass roots reports.

She had been living in Boston the very year when William Lloyd Garrison founded his antislavery magazine, *The Liberator*, and was dragged through the streets on a rope by a "respectable and influential mob of Boston citizens." She read of the 1850 Compromise supported by Daniel Webster and of the blood shed in Kansas over the slavery issue.

In the political campaign of 1856, the new Republican party nominated John C. Frémont as its presidential candidate. For the first time a woman was prominent in campaign slogans and songs—the candidate's wife, Jessie Benton Frémont, daughter of Senator Benton.

> With pride we can point at our own candidate,
> Who doubled his value by taking a mate,
> And who found in his Jessie a treasure more bright
> Than all Mariposa will e'er bring to light.

Jessie had written much of her husband's *Report* of his exploring expedition to California, revealing the golden possibilities of this region to the American public. Frémont was only forty-three years old when he won the nomination with the slogan "Free soil, free speech, and Frémont."

The Democrats chose James Buchanan of Pennsylvania, an experienced politician and "a fine old fossil bachelor" of sixty-five years, who campaigned on the safe policy of holding the Union together—and he won. But slavery was the real issue in the campaign. The popular vote for Buchanan was 1,838,000 but Frémont's was a close 1,340,000, and the Southern states felt threatened. "After 1856 there was real fear in the South and much talk of secession if the election of 1860 should go against them."

The close popular vote indicated how polarized the country was between the slaveholding and the free states.

The Lincoln–Douglas debates brought the issue before the nation again in 1858. Both Lincoln and Douglas were contenders in the next presidential election. But in Godey's *Book* any reference to such controversial subjects was forbidden. Sarah Hale had seen what had happened to the careers of Lydia Maria Child, Grace Greenwood, and others when they aligned themselves publicly on the abolitionist side. Lydia Child had written several useful and popular books and edited a children's magazine until, in 1833, she published *An Appeal in Favor of That Class of Americans Called Africans*, one of the early protests against racial prejudice. Then "old associates departed," Mrs. Child regretted, and she had to resign as editor of the children's magazine.

As early as 1849, the Columbia, South Carolina, *Telegraph* published an angry outburst against the *Lady's Book* because its junior editor, Grace Greenwood, was contributing articles to an abolitionist journal. This, it was suggested, was "an argument against lining Northern pockets with Southern cash." Godey promptly withdrew Grace Greenwood's name from his cover, and the spirited author herself published a card in the newspapers stating that she no longer had any connection of any kind with the *Lady's Book*.

Despite Godey's strict avoidance of political issues, it was Harriet Beecher Stowe, whose short stories the *Lady's Book* had printed, who fueled the intense antislavery feelings that led to the Civil War with her novel, *Uncle Tom's Cabin*. Three hundred thousand copies of this book were purchased in the ten months after its publication in 1852, and the same year several touring companies dramatized the story.

Sarah Hale, a political moderate and a cautious business woman, "permitted" *Northwood* to be reissued in 1852. It was one of a number of books that was published to attempt to counteract the effect of *Uncle Tom's Cabin*. *Northwood* contrasted the two opposing cultures that had grown up side by side in the United States. Mrs. Hale explained in her new preface:

> *Northwood* was written when what is now known as "Abolitionism" first began to disturb seriously the harmony between the South and the North. . . . That it is easier to burn a temple than to build one, and that two wrongs never make one right, are points conceded by all; yet all seem not to have considered what is quite as sure, that fraud and falsehood never promote the cause of goodness, nor can physical force make or keep men free. . . . The great error of those who would sever the Union, rather than see a slave within its borders, is that they forget the master is their brother as well as the servant. . . . Hoping that *Northwood* might in some degree aid in diffusing the true spirit, I have consented to its republication at this time.

The next year she published another novel, *Liberia*, offering what she felt might be a solution to the great problem: First, education of slaves and then the purchase of their freedom. Following this, the freedmen would be sent to join the colony of Liberia in Africa, started by the American Colonization Society in 1820.

Meanwhile, Godey was becoming more determined to keep all controversial issues out of the *Lady's Book*. At a public dinner in March 1856, celebrating the fiftieth volume of the magazine, he said: "I allow no man's religion to be attacked or sneered at, or the subject of politics to be mentioned in my magazine. The first is obnoxious to myself and to the latter the ladies object; and it is my business and pleasure to please them, for to them—God bless the fairest portion of His creation—am I indebted for my success."

Sarah J. Hale and Alice B. Neal were referred to at this dinner as his "accomplished collaborators," Morton McMichael as his mentor and friend for twenty-seven years.

Because of Godey's cautious "no politics" stand, his *Book* missed opportunities for service to the country when the Civil War came. The *Book* did not even echo its own protégée, Dr. Elizabeth Blackwell, when she issued a call for nurses. Sarah J. Hale, the accomplished organizer and publicist, capable of rallying the women of America to give and to serve, was mute. Other women were heard from. The seventy-four-year-old Emma Willard appealed unsuccessfully to South Carolina not to secede. She presented a *Memorial from American Women* to Congress and tried to organize a peace convention, but it was all too late.

Even the ethereal Lydia H. Sigourney had something to say on this subject in her poem "Prejudice Reproved":

> God gave to Africa's sons
> A brow of sable dye;
> And spread the country of their birth
> Beneath a burning sky.
>
> With a cheek of olive He made
> The little Hindoo child;
> And darkly stained the forest tribes,
> That roam our Western wild.
>
> To me He gave a form
> Of fairer, whiter clay;
> But am I, therefore, in his sight,
> Respected more than they?
>
> No;—t'is the hue of *deeds* and *thoughts*
> He traces in his book;

'Tis the complexion of the *heart*
On which He deigns to look.

Not by the tinted cheek,
That fades away so fast,
But by the color of the *soul*,
We shall be judged at last.

When war gripped the country, the circulation of Godey's *Lady's Book* dropped by one third. The "politics are out" decree led many readers to turn to other sources of information. Reporters and artists like Walt Whitman and young Winslow Homer covered the war for *Harper's Weekly* and *Leslie's Illustrated Magazine.* During this period *Harper's Weekly* attained the peak circulation that Godey's *Book* had reached in 1856.

The soldiers read a new form of literature, dime novels, when they could get them. The first one, issued by the firm of Beadle in New York City, was by Ann S. Stephens, Sarah's rival editor of *Peterson's Magazine.* Its orange paper cover bore the title *Malaeska, the Indian Wife of the White Hunter,* and it was an adventure story guaranteed to divert the mind from the two evils of soldiery, boredom and fear.

During the war, Ann Stephens served as vice-president of the Ladies National Covenant, a society for the "suppression of extravagance"; afterwards she compiled a pictorial history of the war.

The January 1861 issue of Godey's *Book* paid tribute to five women who had achieved a fame "justly won," but unsought: Elizabeth Fry, an Englishwoman, renowned for her work in prison reform; Dorothea Dix, New England-born, who worked to improve the lot of the insane, sick, and destitute (she was later made superintendent of the Union nurses in the war); Grace Darling, also English, who, with her father's aid, saved nine men shipwrecked off the Northumberland coast; Mrs. Cornelius Du Bois, of New York City, who established the Nursery and Child's Hospital, "the first of the kind known in our country," to aid the children of the poor; and, finally, Florence Nightingale.

Sarah Hale wrote:

> War is not forever, but the poor will always be with us; sorrow, sickness, destitution and death are the perpetual attendants on fallen humanity. Therefore the mind that has devised means to soften these ever-recurring miseries . . . is indeed of the highest order. This intelligence has been shown by Florence Nightingale in her writings and exertions to organize a new system of hospital treatment, of which experience has already proved the efficacy. For these beneficent services which she has done for her country, nay, for all mankind . . . Miss Nightingale truly deserves what the world tenders her—honor, esteem, love.

In the fall of 1860, Mrs. Hale had reviewed *Notes on Nursing*, Florence Nightingale's new book on practical nursing, urging readers to buy it and study it at once. "Learn what is needed now," she advised. It was as if she could see already the lines of wounded men and hear in the distance the guns and the roar of cannon. "This little volume of eighty pages," she wrote, "is one of the most important works ever put forth by woman; and very few medical books produced by the most eminent men equal it in usefulness and in the good it must initiate and produce for the sick and suffering. . . . We hope to incite every lady who comes to our Table for counsel to study the work and practise its precepts."

Florence Nightingale strongly advocated nurses' training

"to know what are the laws of life and death for men, and what the laws of health for wards." She maintained that women's dress was inappropriate for "any mission or usefulness at all. The fidget of silk and of crinoline, the rattling of keys, the creaking of stays and of shoes, will do a patient more harm than all the medicines in the world will do him good. The noiseless step of woman, the noiseless drapery, are mere figures of speech in this day."

Over the years Godey's editor had promoted the training of women as doctors and nurses, and now those ready and qualified certainly would be needed. Many women, untrained except in caring for their own families, would volunteer for the work—including the young writer Louisa May Alcott. Poet Walt Whitman also went, on his own initiative, to bring comfort and cheer to the wounded soldiers on or near the battlefields. In his notes Whitman mentioned the young women nurses (over 3,000 volunteered to work in hospitals): "They are a help in certain ways. . . . Then it remains to be distinctly said that few or no young ladies, under the irresistible conventions of society, answer the practical requirements of nurses for soldiers. Middle-aged or healthy and good-conditioned elderly women, mothers of children, are always best. . . ." In another note he said, "Mothers full of motherly feeling, and however illiterate but bringing reminiscences of home and the magnetic touch of hands, are the true women nurses. Many of the wounded are between 15 and 20 years of age."

As Louisa Alcott testified, Dorothea Dix kept a vigilant eye on the nurses under her jurisdiction, but it was considered unseemly for women to nurse soldiers at the front.

"Great and important changes are coming on our land; not only is their shadow now over us, but the strong hand of destiny has already shaken many a tower of safety to atoms," declared a Sarah Hale editorial, daring for the nonpolitical *Lady's Book*. Quoting a letter from a woman in Pennsylvania that actually referred to the war, the bereaved, and to "this strange crisis," it suggested that widows and mothers who are bereft "might be allowed" to make a living as post mistresses, especially in villages and small towns. They might also be permitted to do bookkeeping, and educated young women could be trained to this work. Sarah Hale appealed to men to aid women in making a livelihood in this way. Thus, little by little, and "gently," the editor was helping to expand the employment of women.

Already, through her efforts and those of other persevering women, the professions of teaching, medicine, and literature were opened to women. In more mundane employments, an 1845 catalog listed women in jobs such as the making of gloves, glue, snuff, and cigars; as laundresses, stereotypers, department store clerks, waitresses. Typesetting by the mid-1850s was increasingly done by women. Pioneers such as Antoinette Browne and the Grimké sisters had walked boldly to the pulpit and the lecture platform.

In 1860, "for her distinguished services in the cause of female education," Sarah J. Hale was awarded a special medal from the Baltimore Female College, one of the largest colleges for women in the country.

It would have been hard indeed for a woman like Mrs. Hale to withhold her opinion of the war. Perhaps this is why she devoted herself during the war years to the development of Vassar College and other constructive projects. Including in the *Lady's Book* stories about the Revolution, both from the northern and southern states, she had striven to awaken Americans to their heritage. Earlier she had been active in raising funds to restore Mount Vernon, Washington's home on the Potomac, as a national shrine. Many such campaigns of restoration and renovation have saved other historic buildings, battlegrounds, and parks since then, so that our generation and future ones may gain a sense of their past, their heritage. Sarah Josepha Hale zealously promoted and believed in these projects.

Colonel Charles Hunter, her grandson, said that Mrs. Hale "deplored the Civil War. She agonized over it. For she was sure that education and time would have solved the problem, freed the slaves and adjusted the economic controversy without sacrifice of life."

Postscript: On Old Friends

By the end of the war Sarah Hale and Louis Godey were in their late seventies. They had seen much change and helped to bring about some themselves. Friend after friend had disappeared from the scene. Thomas Buchanan Read, the poet-artist, for one, after working hard for the Union cause throughout the war, left for Italy, where he lived until 1872. His poems, "Sheridan's Ride" and 'The Eagle and the Vulture," called forth by the war, live on in anthologies.

N. P. Willis, master of the "graceful trifle" in literature, lived and wrote in Idlewild, his specially designed Gothic residence at Cornwall-on-the-Hudson, New York, until, during the war, he went to Washington as correspondent for his newspaper. He died at Idlewild on January 20, 1867.

Eliza Leslie became a Philadelphia institution years before her death at the age of seventy; she was painted by Thomas Sully; her books on cookery and etiquette became steady sellers, bringing her an income that she was overgenerous in sharing.

Lydia Sigourney pressed on to complete sixty-seven books in all, including a posthumously published *Letters of Life* (1866), a strange title for one whose work so often seemed to celebrate death. She had few illusions concerning her net literary worth. "If there is any kitchen in Parnassus, my Muse has surely officiated there as a woman of all work and an aproned waiter," she wrote.

In Sarah's own family several of her children had predeceased her. In 1863 her daughter and namesake, Sarah Josepha Hale, died at her desk between two recitation periods. Her brother William George Hale died in New Orleans in 1876 of malarial fever. Horatio Hale, who, like William, had become a member of the bar, lived in Ontario, Canada, with his family. He devoted his time partly to his profession, partly to management of the estate of his father-in-law, William Pugh, who owned a large tract of land in Clinton, Ontario, and partly to his study of the Indian tribes of Canada and the United States. His work, *The Iroquois Book of Rites*, appeared in 1883, and remains in print today. Mr. Hale, like his distinguished mother, was active in urging the admission of girls to high schools, to give them the same advantages as boys.

Her family could scarcely recall a time when Sarah Hale was not busy—reading or writing at her large table desk, yet she always warmly welcomed old friends. A letter of August 6, 1873, written in her own hand, tells much:

> I wish we could meet and talk half an hour; this attempt to write with my weak eyes is not pleasant, and yet I cannot dictate what I desire to say to you, my beloved friend.—Pardon my delay. My sight has so far improved that I am able to scribble, and I am thankful. This joy was enhanced when I received your kind message of love and learned that new ties of family happiness were unfolding for you in the happiness of your darling Emily. Should I write of your good and lovely daughter as I feel she deserves to be praised, it would surely close by my saying that no man could be found worthy of her love.
>
> And yet I trust that she has been appreciated by a noble-minded and just man who will obey the great Apostle's injunction and "love his wife as himself." I am a believer in love marriages, and—as you say they have been long acquainted . . . I feel sure of

their belief in my theory. So I congratulate you, my dear friend, and send my fervent wishes for the happiness of your daughter. One objection I must urge: I cannot feel reconciled to the loss of my dear Emily . . . from my list of young friends in Philadelphia. Could not the Rev. Mr. L_____ be settled over some parish in our City of Homes and Churches?

But I forget that my blind writing is not easy reading and yet this pleasure of using my own pen even imperfectly as this letter shows, is a pleasure to me for which I am devoutly thankful. In truth, my life is a (continuous?) thanksgiving. My health is excellent. Our residence in this home of the Rev. Dr. Hodge has been delightful. The house is large and surrounded by great green trees—a beautiful green lawn in front, and under the roof we find all appliances for household comfort. We have our own servants, Richard, his wife and their dear little baby are with us—and thus *four generations* are here together in the enjoyment of the best blessings of home life, health, comfort, peace and love.

Pray write soon, that I may know you get my letter.

We shall return to the city (D.V.) on the 28th. When you reach the same haven of straight streets come to *Locust* Street or let me know where to find you.

Enclosed is a page of mine from the *Lady's Book*. I hope this will interest you who have been so truly blessed in your good sons.—Well now you have a quartette of grandsons. May they all be trained as their fathers were to join the songs of angels in Heaven—where your *one, dear departed* is now rejoicing in glory.

Give my heart's love to your daughter and believe me ever

> Your affectionate friend,
> Sarah Josepha Hale.

(Datelined Princeton, N. J., Aug. 6th, 1873.)

17

"An Enviable Immortality"

The closest surviving competitor to Godey's *Book* after the war was *Peterson's Magazine* (1842–1898), also published in Philadelphia. Charles J. Peterson had been a partner in the *Saturday Evening Post* and later done some editing on *Graham's Magazine.*

Ann S. Stephens was co-editor of *Peterson's* from 1842 to 1853. Like Sarah J. Hale, she had edited a magazine in New England, the *Portland* (Maine) *Magazine,* published by her husband. Her story, "Mary Derwent," had won a prize, and in 1854 she wrote a sensational novel, *Fashion and Famine,* contrasting city and country life and centering on a murder trial. She had also contributed occasionally to Godey's *Book* and worked on *Graham's Magazine.* In 1856 she launched *Mrs. Stephens' Illustrated New Monthly,* which in two years merged with the better-known *Peterson's.* While the publisher claimed this was not just a lady's magazine, "but a *national* one also," its contents were mainly directed to women and it featured the serialized stories of Ann Stephens. For some years the two magazines, *Godey's* and *Peterson's,* had raced neck and neck. Ann Stephens wrote one serialized story a year, which, neatly, ran in *Peterson's* from January through the December number. These serials were then issued in book form, several as dime novels. Peterson boasted: "Mrs. Stephens has no rival in American literature, in the higher walks of passionate fiction." He even compared her to Sir Walter Scott!

Sarah Hale, in *Woman's Record,* called her one of the most successful magazine writers of the day and quoted Peterson's description of her prose, which poured out "glowing like molten lava." Even Poe regarded her as a power in the magazine world.

By the beginning of the Civil War, *Peterson's Magazine* was overtaking Godey's *Book* in circulation. But it carried fewer pages during the war; these were restored, together with steel engravings and colored fashion plates, when peace came.

In his Arm-Chair column in July 1861, Godey marked the thirty-second year of his *Book's* existence and printed a deserved tribute to Sarah Hale from the *Vandalia Democrat;* it read, in part:

> The lady editor of Godey's Lady's Book has won for herself an enviable immortality, an immortality not of theory, but of living worth and excellence . . . in the strength and maturity of womanhood, in the vigor of life, and—it may be—in her declining years she speaks through the press to the same hearts she gladdened in youth, dispensing . . . the priceless treasures of her own rich laden mind, exquisite in taste, full in all the acquirements that grace and adorn the character of woman. She needs no marble monument to perpetuate her name, for upon millions of hearts is written:

> To the Memory of Sarah Josepha Hale

During the war, Godey claimed to have received subscriptions from the army, but it took time to rebuild the circulation lost in the Southern states. Conditions there during the war and the early days of Reconstruction were desolate. Few could afford to indulge in Godey's fashions, model cottages, and embroideries, or had any interest in them.

Literature was now closer to life—in the war stories of Ambrose Bierce; *Life in the Iron Mills* by Rebecca Harding Davis (1861); or the humorous tales of Western life by Edward Eggleston, whose *Hoosier Schoolmaster* Sarah Hale called "the liveliest book of the month," in March 1872.

For some years, of course, Dickens's writings had had a strong influence on Americans' taste in literature. He knew how to dramatize the problems of the industrial age, the exploitation of children, the toils and inequities of the law. Common people related to his characters. His portrait by Daniel Maclise had been widely published and on his first visit to the United States in 1842, wherever he went people recognized him and rushed up to shake his hand.

Despite his uncomplimentary views on the United States, revealed with the publication of his *American Notes* and *Martin Chuzzlewit*, Dickens's works were republished in edition after edition here. In 1858 Sarah Hale praised a new twenty-five-volume edition of Dickens, citing his original wit and surprising turns of phrase. His stories, she felt, "may be read aloud in any circle and put without fear in the hands of the young. . . . Mr. Peterson's new edition [with its] good clear type and humorous pictures gives a double zest to the perusal." Dickens's influence extended into the seventies, even touching the work of Bret Harte.

Literary taste was dulled during the post-Civil War decade. Critics have called it "the Brown Decade" and "the Dreadful Decade." The dime novel and folksy rhymes like those of Will Carleton and James Whitcomb Riley were in tune with the times. The vigorous new writing was coming from the West—from Mark Twain, who got educated in a newspaper office and as a Mississippi River pilot, and Bret Harte, also of the newspaper and printing trade. Americans began to realize how diverse their society and their land areas really were, as a result of this new writing. From the Sierras, from San Francisco (fast built by Gold Rushers), from Chicago, "hog butcher for the world," from the dusty plains of the West and the sleepy small towns where they said "it warn't" and "I knowed" writers tried to give the sound of the talkers of America, the voices, the tall tale tellers, the people who were making all the stories happen! America was singing, at last, of herself!

Peterson's Magazine continued to thrive—and it, too, published colored fashion plates and sold for only two dollars a year, while *Godey's* was three dollars. The newer magazines—*Harper's Weekly* (founded in 1850), the *Atlantic Monthly* (1857), and *Putnam's* (1853)—were competing for both new and established writers.

Through the late sixties and into the seventies *Godey's* continued to publish Marion Harland, Mary W. Janvrin, Fitz-Greene Halleck, and Catherine M. Sedgwick, "the most popular American female novelist before Harriet Beecher Stowe." *Godey's* even began a series of cartoons, "Miss Lollipop's Party," satirizing the social life of the 1870s. About this time Frances E. Hodgson contributed to Godey's *Book*. She later wrote the children's favorites *The Secret Garden*, *Little Lord Fauntleroy*, and *The Little Princess*, all still in print.

During these years Godey's *Book* was more elaborate than ever in color lithography, engraved portraits, stenciled or transfer designs for embroideries, patchwork patterns, fashions in both color and black-and-white. Advertisements were much more prominent and numerous, evidently helping to pay for the lavish illustrations. The ads themselves were bolder and were illustrated. Marion Harland's serialized stories seemed to go on forever.

Early in 1870, the editor again spoke out on women's role.

Having progressed so far in the past twenty years, she said, "there seems now some fear lest [woman] should, in her eagerness to show the world what she can do, aim rather at doing men's work as the best proof of her ability. This would be a serious mistake. . . ." And Sarah Hale restated her belief that woman has a special role, above and beyond the political or material. A year or two later she expressed alarm at the "dangerous boon" asked by women who wanted the right to vote. These "complainers represent a very small fraction of American women." Still, in 1871, she felt that women could perform useful work on school boards. . . . "American women in general, even those who are most eager in demanding what they deem the 'rights' of their sex, have failed to comprehend their duties in regard to the schools in which their sons and daughters are educated." In this respect she was far in advance of her age, though in the matter of women's right to vote she was curiously conservative.

Her *Woman's Record* went into its third edition, revised and enlarged, in 1870 and reviews of it were reprinted in *Godey's* Arm Chair column.

According to letters from readers of Godey's *Book*, they found a "constant freshness of interest" in the magazine at this time, but a comparison of, say, a January 1872 issue with a January issue of ten years before would not reveal a great difference in general tone and subject matter. The model homes had become grander suburban residences and more attention was given to the sciences and such topics as "Worrying" or "The Tyranny of Temper in the Home," but *Godey's* seemed nonetheless to be drifting into a repetitious old age. The familiar appearance of its pages may have been reassuring to a devoted readership, but Godey's own column was strangely silent on the circulation figure, while devoting much space to letters from subscribers praising the *Book.* The *Journal* of El Paso, Illinois, comments: "What glorious *young* old people Godey and Mrs. Hale must be. Here are forty-two years they have been consecutively publishing the *Lady's Book*, and this year it displays more vim, and vigor, and *freshness* than it did thirty years ago. . . ."

However, the literary department lacked its former vitality. Many stories were unsigned or signed only with initials, with a resulting loss of the color and personality that flavored the earlier years. The cheeriest departments in these later issues are the juvenile department, with its games and riddles and activities, and the gardening columns. Sarah Hale's Editor's Table continued to have a lively quality, but for the most part the word "predictable" best described this magazine, which had weathered the financial and political storms of the nation but seemed now to be settling into a complacent routine.

Having completed her fiftieth year as an editor, Sarah Josepha Hale, at the age of eighty-nine, gracefully withdrew after the management of *Godey's Book* was reorganized in 1877. "Have we done good?" was the question she asked of her long editorship—and of her life.

The following year Louis A. Godey died quietly, while reading in his arm chair. Retirement lasted only about a year for his friend and associate, Sarah Hale. On her ninetieth birthday she read aloud to her family a new poem she had written:

> Growing old! growing old! Do they say it of *me*?
>   Do they hint my fine fancies are faded and fled?
> That my garden of life, like the winter-swept tree,
>   Is frozen and dying, or fallen and dead?
>
> Is the heart growing old, when each beautiful thing,
>   Like a landscape at eve, looks more tenderly bright,
> And love sweeter seems, as the bird's wand'ring wing
>   Draws nearer her nest at the coming of night?

The image of the winter-swept tree is an apt one. Sarah Hale had always taken special notice of the sturdy pine trees that grew on her birthplace farm. Like one of those tall pines, she always sought to stand erect, with a will and a mind of her own.

Appendixes

Announcement in Godey's Arm Chair
column for February, 1857:

Mrs. Hale's Books

Inquiries are made for the works of the editress of the Lady's Book. Mr. Godey will send any one or all the books in question at the prices named below.

1. *Woman's Record; a Biographical Dictionary of all Distinguished Women from the Creation to A.D. 1854.* Arranged in Four Eras. With Selections from Feminine Writers of every Age. Illustrated by two hundred and thirty Portraits. Second Edition, revised. Large octavo, pp. 912. Price in cloth $5.00
2. *Northwood; or, Life, North and South.* Illustrated . 1.00
3. *Three Hours; or, the Vigil of Love.* (Poems) 1.00
4. *Liberia; or, Mr. Peyton's Experiments* 75
5. *The Bible Reading-Book;* containing such portions of the Old and New Testaments as form a Connected Narrative, in the exact words of Scripture, and in the Order of the Sacred Books, of God's Dealings with Man, and Man's Duties to God. With the Chronology arranged, and an Index 75

6. *The White Veil; a Bridal Gift.* Elegantly Illustrated . 4.50
7. *The Ladies' New Book of Cookery* 1.00
8. *The Ladies' New Household Receipt-Book;* containing Maxims, Directions, and Specifics for
   promoting Health, Comfort, and Improvement in
   the Homes of the People 1.00
9. *Flora's Interpreter.* Illustrated 1.25
10. *Selections from Letters of Madame de Sevigné* 1.25
11. *Selections from Letters of Lady Mary Wortley
    Montagu* 1.25
12. *Sketches of American Character* 1.00

    Twelve works complete for $19.75

    Whoever will remit the money (letter post-paid) to the editors of the Lady's Book shall be furnished with any one of the above volumes at the price stated, without expense of postage on the book. Should the whole series be ordered, there will be a deduction of one dollar and seventy-five cents.

Address: L. A. Godey
No. 113 Chestnut Street, Philadelphia.

Sarah J. Hale books currently in print:

Liberia, Or, Mr. Peyton's Experiments. 1853. Reprint. Boston: Gregg Press, 1969.

Manners: Happy Homes & Good Society All the Year Round. 1868. Reprint. New York: Arno Press, 1972.

Northwood. 1852 Facsimile edition. Freeport, N.Y.: Books for Libraries, 1974.

Woman's Record; or, Sketches of All Distinguished Women from "the Beginning" till A.D. 1850. 1853. Reprint. Ann Arbor, Mich.: Finch Press.

Postscript

In 1956 friends of the Richards Library in Newport, New Hampshire, Sarah Josepha Hale's birthplace, established an award in her honor. A medal is given each year to a prominent author associated with New England through work or residence. Among those so far honored are: Robert Frost, John P. Marquand, Archibald MacLeish, Mary Ellen Chase, Mark Van Doren, Catherine Drinker Bowen, David McCord, John Hersey, Ogden Nash, Louis Untermeyer, Raymond Holden, Robert Lowell, John Kenneth Galbraith, Richard Wilbur, Lawrence Thompson, Elizabeth Yates, Norman Cousins, May Sarton, Henry Steele Commager, and Edwin Way Teale.

On October 19, 1963, Americans met in Clinton, Ontario, Canada, to honor Horatio Emmons Hale, who was described as "the greatest scholar in Canada in the nineteenth century." Tribute was paid to him in English and in the Iroquois language by representatives of the United States and Canadian governments and of the Six Nations. A plaque bearing the following permanent tribute to Horatio Hale was unveiled:

HORATIO EMMONS HALE
1817–1896

One of North America's pioneer ethnologists and linguists, Hale practised law in Clinton 1856–1896.

Born in New Hampshire, he graduated from Harvard in 1837 and accompanied the Wilkes Expedition to the Pacific 1838–1842. His contribution to the Narrative of that voyage is one of the basic sources for Polynesian ethnology. Hale discovered that the Tutelos near Brantford, fugitives from North Carolina, belonged to the Siouan family and identified the Cherokees of the Carolinas as linguistically Iroquoian. His intensive study of the languages and customs of the Six Nations of the Grand River culminated in his classic work, "An Iroquois Book of Rites," published in 1883.

Archaeological and Historic Sites Board on Ontario

Books for Further Reading

Bell, E. Moberly. *Storming the Citadel, The Rise of the Woman Doctor*. London: Constable & Co., Ltd., 1953.

Bird, Caroline, with Briller, Sara Welles. *Born Female, The High Cost of Keeping Women Down*. New York: David McKay Co., Inc., 1968.

Bolton, Sarah Knowles. *Famous Leaders among Women*. New York: Thomas Y. Crowell Co., 1895. Books for Libraries, facsimile edition.

Burnett, Constance Buel. Happily Ever After, a Portrait of *Frances Hodgson Burnett*. New York: Vanguard Press, Inc., 1965.

Cantwell, Robert. *Famous American Men of Letters*. New York: Dodd, Mead & Co., 1956.

Delgado, Alan. *Florence Nightingale*. London: George G. Harrap & Co., 1970.

Hale, Edward Everett. *A New England Boyhood*. Boston: Little, Brown & Co., 1927.

Henderson, Daniel M. *Hidden Coasts*. New York: William Sloane Associates, 1953. A biography of Charles Wilkes.

Holmes, Oliver Wendell. *Poetical Works of Oliver Wendell Holmes*. Boston: Houghton, Mifflin Company.

Larcom, Lucy. *A New England Girlhood*. New York: Corinth Books, 1961.

Poe, Edgar Allan. *Complete Stories and Poems of Edgar Allan Poe*. New York: Doubleday & Co., 1966.

Stern, Madeleine B. *We the Women, Career Firsts of Nineteenth Century America.* New York: Schulte Publishing Company, 1963.

Stern, Philip Van Doren. *Edgar Allan Poe, Visitor from the Night of Time.* New York: Thomas Y. Crowell Co., 1973.

Index

Abolitionism, 123
Abolitionists, 70, 83, 121
Aimée-Martin, L., 82
"Al Aaraaf," 60
Alcott, Louisa May, 67, 127
Alcott, William A., 84
Allen, Hervey, 61
Allston, Washington, 42
American Ladies' Magazine, 24, 26, 30, 31, 40, 42, 45, 50–53, 67, 78; on fashions, 73; on girls' education, 82; on physiology, 84; purchased by Godey, 53
American literature, 30–31, 60, 70, 135–136
American Notes, 135
American Philosophical Society, 58
Anesthesia, 87–88
Annuals, 27, 59, 70
Antarctica, 55, 61
Antislavery. *See* Abolitionists
Appeal in Favor of That Class of Americans Called Africans, 122
Arthur, T. S., 70
Atlantic Monthly, 136
Autocrat of the Breakfast Table, 30
Avery, Alida C., 112

Baillie, Joanna, 72
Baldwin, Loammi, 42
Baltimore Female College, 128

Barbauld, Mrs. A. L., 82
Bierce, Ambrose, 135
Blackwell, Elizabeth, 85, 124
Blackwell sisters, 86, 90
Blake, George, 42
Blake, John Lauris, 24, 28–29
Bloomer, Amelia, 75
Boston, 25–27, 29, 35, 59, 70, 121
Boston Academy of Music, 26
Boston Athenaeum, 25, 42, 83
Boston Institution for the Blind, 50
Boston Patriot, 40
Boston Port Society, 36
Boston schools, 36, 81–82
Brackenridge, William D., 55
Bowles and Dearborn, 21
Browne, Antoinette, 128
Buchanan, James, 121
Buell, Charles, 12, 14, 19, 35
Buell, Gordon, 11, 12, 14–15, 22
Buell, Horatio, 11, 13, 14, 16, 17, 19, 20
Buell, Martha, 11, 12, 17
Buell, Martha Whittlesey, 11–12, 15, 17, 22
"Building of the Ship," 109
Bulfinch, Charles, 26
Bunker Hill Monument, 26, 40–49; Fair, 44–49; *The Monument*, 46–48
Burnett, Frances Hodgson, 67–68, 136

Index

"Cacoethes Scribendi," 64–65
California, 57, 120, 121
Calisthenics, 74–75, 80
Carey, Matthew, 60
Carleton, Will, 135
"Cask of Amontillado," 104
"Chambered Nautilus," 30
Chambers, W. B., 25
Channing, William Ellery, 26
"Charcoal Sketches," 64
Charlestown, Mass., 40, 41
Child, Lydia Maria, 31, 51, 102, 122
Children's reading, 82, 100
Civil War, 111, 117, 121, 122, 124, 128, 129, 134
Clarke, Sarah Freeman, 83
Columbia River, 55, 61
Complete Dictionary of Poetical Quotations, 108
Constitution (ship), 44
Constitution (U.S.), 114, 117
Cooper, James Fenimore, 70
Copyright law, 29, 61, 71
Couthouy, Joseph P., 55
Critical Dictionary of English Literature, 108

Dana, James Dwight, 55
Dana, Richard Henry, 57, 83
Dancing, 74
Darley, F. O. C., 59
Darling, Grace, 126
Dartmouth College, 13, 14, 16
Davis, Rebecca Harding, 135
Dearborn, H. A. S., 41, 43
Dearborn, Henry, 41
Dickens, Charles, 32, 39, 56, 135
Dickinson, Emily, 80–81
Dime novels, 125, 133, 135
Divorce, 91, 92
Dix, Dorothea, 125, 127
Domestic science, 112
Douglas, Stephen A., 122
Douglass, Frederick, 89
DuBois, Mrs. Cornelius, 126

Edgeworth, Maria, 72
Eggleston, Edward, 135
Eliot, George, 13
Ellett, Elizabeth F., 109
Emerson, Ralph Waldo, 83
English, Thomas Dunn, 102–103
Engravings, 71–72, 75, 76, 136
Ethnography and Philology of the U.S. Exploring Expedition, 96
Everett, Edward, 26, 43

Factories of New England, 57, 66, 67, 78
Familiar Quotations, 109
Fashion, 72–73, 79
Fashion and Famine, 133
Fashion plates, 50, 71, 72, 75, 136
Female, use of word, 112–113
Female Medical College of Philadelphia, 86
Female Medical Education Society (Boston), 86
Female Prose Writers of America, 107
Female seminaries, 79–80
Fern, Fanny, 70
Finley, Ruth, 105
Fiske, Catherine, 79
Flora's Interpreter, 108
Florida, 54
Fourth of July, 97–98
Franklin, Benjamin, 58
Fremont, Jessie Benton, 121
Fremont, John C., 121
French fashion terms, 73
Fry, Elizabeth, 125

Garrison, William Lloyd, 121
Gates, Horatio, 13
"Gathering Song," 97–98
Geneva College (N.Y.), 85
Genius of Oblivion, 21
Glens Falls, N.Y., 17, 20
Godey, Louise E., 50, 52–56, 59, 61, 69, 75–76, 100, 105, 129, 138

Goodrich, Samuel G., 27–28
Graham, George Rex, 62
Graham's Magazine, 60, 66–67, 70, 76, 78, 133
Greenwood, Grace, 70, 122
Grimké sisters, 128
Guild, N.H., 16

Hale, David, 16, 17, 19, 20–22
Hale, David Emerson, 31, 54, 55–56, 60
Hale, Frances Ann, 54, 95
Hale, Hannah, 20
Hale, Horatio, 20, 31, 54–58, 96–97, 99, 130
Hale, Sarah Josepha (daughter), 54, 95, 99–100, 129–130
Hale, Sarah Josepha (Buell): birth-place, 11; education, 11–14, 16; school teacher, 16; writes verse, 16; wedding, 17–19; Connecticut forebears, 12, 97; appearance, 16, 25, 61; on marriage, 19; children, 20, 23, 25, 26, 31; millinery business, 20–21; poems published, 21, 26–27, 66, 82; Boston editorship, 25–31, 53; objectives, 23, 26, 31, 105; en-courages American writers, 30; founds Seaman's Aid Society, 35; public relations skills, 46; move to Philadelphia, 55–56; editorial duties, 63, 66, 69; views on fashion, 72–74; promotes union of states, 98, 109, 117, 119, 120, 123; receives medal, 128; on woman's role, 137–138; promotes restorations, 128; "Lines" to a granddaughter, 100; views on Civil War, 129; on dancing, 74; on woman's rights, 89–92; on education for women, 78–83, 128; women's hygiene, 84; advice to parents, 82; tribute to, 134; withdraws from *Lady's Book*, 138; poems quoted, 17, 19–20, 97–98, 100, 138

Hale, William, 20, 55–56, 96, 99, 130
Halleck, Fitz-Greene, 136
Harland, Marion, 136
Harper's Weekly, 125, 136
Hart, John S., 107–108
Harte, Bret, 135
Harvard College, 25, 31, 54, 55, 56
Harvard Medical School, 85
Haven's Coffee-room, 29
Hawthorne, Nathaniel, 29, 65, 70, 102, 104
"Hearts and Diamonds," 68
"Heroic Women of the Revolution," 109
History of Boston, 26
History of the American Revolution, 13
Hodgson, Frances. *See* Burnett, Frances Hodgson
Holmes, Oliver Wendell, 27, 30, 44, 78, 85
Homer, Winslow, 125
Homestead Laws, 106
Hoosier Schoolmaster, 135
Housing, low-rent, 38
Happy to Be Happy, 59
Hunt, Harriot Keziah, 85
Hunter, Charles, 129
Hunter, Lewis Boudinot, 95, 100
Hunter, Richard, 111, 131

Inventions, 109–110
Iroquois Book of Rites, 130

James, Henry, 60
Janvrin, Mary W., 136
Jefferson, Thomas, 13
Johnson, Andrew, 118
Juvenile Lyre, 27
Juvenile Miscellany, 31

Ladies' Magazine. *See American Ladies' Magazine*

Index

Ladies' Medical Missionary Society, 85–86

Lady of Godey's, 105

Lady's Book (Godey's), 53–54, 65, 67; competition, 76, 133, 136; contributors, 59, 60, 63–64, 68, 70, 101; culinary dept., 117; editorial policy, 54, 63, 69, 120–121, 123; encourages inventions, 109–110; engravings, 71–72; features, 74–75; inspiring to women, 78, 105–106; in Civil War, 124–125, 127–128, 134–135; on woman's rights, 89–91, 106; Poe's opinion of, 76; post-Civil War, 136–138; praised, 137–138; prepared by women, 71; reasons for success, 70–71; services, 109, 110; staff, 63–44; subscriptions, 75, 101, 109, 125, 134, 137; tribute to women, 125–126

Lafayette, Marquis de, 24, 26

Larcom, Lucy, 66, 78

Lawrence, Amos, 43, 44, 49

Legal Rights, Liabilities, etc. of Women, 91

Leslie, Charles Robert, 64, 71

Leslie, Eliza, 56, 63, 64, 129

Leslie's Illustrated Magazine, 125

Letters of Life, 129

Letters to Mothers, 64

Letters to Young Ladies, 59

Leutze, E. G., 71

Liberator, 121

Liberia, 22, 123

Liberia, 123

Life in the Iron Mills, 135

Lincoln, Abraham, 117–118, 122

Lind, Jenny, 74

Literati articles, 30, 101–104

Livett & Parker's pen, 29

Longfellow, Henry Wadsworth, 26, 29, 78, 102, 109

Lowell Institute lectures, 83

Lowell Offering, 78

Lyman, Hannah W., 112

Lyon, Mary, 24, 80–81

McGuffey's *Readers*, 82

McMichael, Morton, 64, 124

Magazine, 54

Magazines for women, 24, 50–54, 67, 133

Malaeska, 125

Manners, 74, 91, 118

Mansfield, Edward D., 91

Married Women's Property Bill, 92

Married women's rights, 38, 91–93

Martin Chuzzlewit, 135

"Mary's Lamb," 16, 27

Mason, Lowell, 26–27

Massachusetts General Hospital, 87

Massachusetts Medical College, 88

Mastodon, 58

Methodist Church, Board, 87

Mexico, 57, 96, 99

Miller, Elizabeth Smith, 75

Miss Leslie's Magazine, 64

Mitchell, Maria, 112

Mitford, Mary Russell, 72

Monument, The, 46–48

Morse, S. F. B., 71

Morton, William Thomas, 87–88

Mott, Lucretia, 89

Mount, W. S., 71

Mount Holyoke College, 24, 80–81

Mount Vernon, 109, 128

Mrs. Stephens' Illustrated New Monthly, 133

"Mrs. Washington Potts," 64

Mysteries of Udolpho, 13

Neal, Alice B., 64, 124

Neal, Joseph C., 64

Needlework instruction, 36

New England training, 66

Hew Hampshire Spectator, 52

New York (city), 65, 70, 126
New York Infirmary for Women and
    Children, 86
New York Mirror, 66, 70, 103
Newport, N.H., 11, 12, 15–17, 97–98
Nightingale, Florence, 126
Normal schools, 82, 94, 106
North American Review, 25, 42
Northwood, 21–22, 24, 113, 122–123
Northwood, N.H., 28
Norton, Caroline, 92–93
Nursery and Child's Hospital (NYC),
    126
Nurses' training, 84, 126–127

Old Corner Bookstore, 29
"Old Ironsides," 44
Oregon Territory, 56–57, 96

Parkman, Francis, 26
Peacock (ship), 61
Peale, Charles Willson, 55, 58
Peale, Titian, 55, 58
Pennsylvania Freeman, 59
Peterson, Charles J., 133
Peterson's Magazine, 67, 125, 133,
    136
Philadelphia, 58–59, 60–62, 65
Phillips Academy, 28
Phrenology, 50
Physical Education. *See* Calisthenics
Pickering, Charles, 55
Pilgrim's Progress, 13
Poe, Edgar Allan, 27, 30, 59, 60–61,
    70, 76, 78, 101–105, 134
Poe, Virginia, 60, 61, 104
Poems for Our Children, 26
Political campaign, 1856, 121–122
Polk, James Knox, 120
Poverty, 35, 36
Prescott, William, 47
Pugh, William, 130
Putnam's Magazine, 136

Quincy Hall, 46–48
Quincy, Josiah, 82

Radcliffe, Ann, 13
Railroad, 97
Ramsay, Nathaniel, 13
Read, Thomas Buchanan, 60, 70, 129
Religion and politics, 54, 123
Republic of America, 24
Revolutionary War, 12, 13, 128
Riley, James Whitcomb, 135
Rising Sun (inn), 15, 16, 17
Roussel's, 59

San Francisco, 56, 57, 136
Sartain, John, 59
Saybrook, Conn., 12
Seaman's Aid Society, 35–39
Seaman's Home, 37–38
Seaman's Society Library, 37
Seamen's Bethel, 32–35, 37, 39
Seamen's boardinghouses, 37
Sedgwick, Catherine, 51, 66, 136
Seminole Indians, 54
Sewing machine, 109
Shelley, Percy Bysshe, 30
Sigourney, Lydia, 51, 59–60, 63–64,
    66, 70, 95, 124–125, 129
Simms, William Gilmore, 70
Slavery, 22, 113, 114, 120, 121–123,
    129
Slop shops, 36, 37
Snow, Caleb, 26
"Spirit of the North," 59
Sports for women, 74
Stagecoach travel, 99
Stanton, Elizabeth Cady, 89, 92
Stark, John, 41
Stephens, Ann S., 125, 133–134
Stowe, Harriet Beecher, 22, 73, 78,
    122, 136
Strauss, Johann, 74
Stuart, Gilbert, 42

Index

Sugar River, N.H., 11, 17
Sullivan, William, 42
Sully, Thomas, 59, 71, 129
Swain, Clara A., 87

Tales of Peter Parley, 27–28
Taylor, Deborah Millet, 32, 35
Taylor, Edward T., 32–35
Teacher training, 82, 94, 95, 106
Tennessee, 67
Texas, 96, 99, 120
Thanksgiving, 14, 98, 113–119
Thanksgiving dinner, 114–117
Ticknor, George, 41, 42
Ticknor, William, 28, 29
Token, The, 70
Touro, Judah, 44, 49
Traits of American Life, 53, 72
Troy, N.Y., 24
Troy Female Seminary, 24, 54, 74,
    81, 95
Tudor, William, 42
Twain, Mark, 135
Two Years Before the Mast, 57
Typewriter, 110, 114

U.S. Exploring Expedition, 55, 56–57,
    58, 61, 96
Uncle Tom's Cabin, 22, 122

Vassar, Matthew, 111, 113
Vassar College, 111–113, 128
Victoria (queen), 72, 74

Warner, Susan, 67
Warren, John C., 41
Warren, Joseph, 41, 42, 46
Warville, Brissot de, 15
Washing machine, 110
Washington, George, 13, 73, 108,
    114, 117

Webster, Daniel, 24, 41, 42, 121
Weir, R. W., 71
West, 65, 66, 78, 135–136
West Point, 31, 60
Whisper to a Bride, 63
Whitcher, Miriam Berry, 64
Whitman, Walt, 34, 125, 127
Whittier, John Greenleaf, 26, 59
Wilkes, Charles, 55, 56
Willard, Emma, 24, 51, 54, 79, 81, 95,
    100, 124
Willard, Solomon, 42
Willard Association for the Mutual
    Development of Female
    Teachers, 95
Willis, Nathaniel Parker, 70, 129
Woman's Record, 107–108, 134, 137
Woman's rights, 89, 90, 137
Women: as breadwinners, 64, 128; as
    nurses, 84, 127–128; Bunker Hill
    Monument and, 42–43, 44–45;
    defy conventions, 65–66;
    education for, 26, 28, 54, 66, 78–
    83, 89, 90, 94, 106, 111;
    education of children, 90;
    freedom for, 83; in home, 12, 54,
    90–92; in medicine, 85–87; in
    professions, 128; in U.S., 84, 91;
    influence of, 65, 79, 83, 91, 94;
    on school boards, 137; right to
    vote, 89, 91, 137; vocations, 14,
    67, 91–92, 106, 128; wages, 37,
    67
Women writers, 51, 59, 65–67, 72,
    134
Women's health, 74, 84–88
Women's Rights Convention, 89
Woods, Delia F., 112
Wright, Frances, 74

Youth's Companion, 70

Zakrewska, Marie, 86

Lewis & Clark College - Watzek Library

3 5209 00811 8818